Meant *for* More

Dear Stephanie —
Never underestimate
the effect of even the
smallest act of kindness!
Karen

Meant for More

FOLLOWING YOUR HEART AND FINDING YOUR PURPOSE

KAREN OLSON

DIAMOND PRESS

Copyright © 2024 by Karen Olson

All rights reserved. Printed and bound in the United States of America. No part of this book may be reproduced or transmitted in any form by any means, electronic or mechanical, including photocopying, recording, or by an information storage and retrieval system—without permission in writing from the publisher, except by a reviewer, who may quote brief passages in a review.

This book is not intended to be a substitute for medical advice from a physician. The reader should regularly consult a physician in all matters relating to his or her health, and particularly in respect to any symptoms that may require a diagnosis or medical attention.

This is a memoir, and the events and experiences detailed in it have been presented as the author currently remembers them, to the best of her ability. Some names and identifying details have been changed to protect the privacy of individuals.

Published by Diamond Press, Springfield, NJ
karenolsonauthor.com
meantformorebook.org

Cover design: David Fassett

ISBN (paperback): 979-8-9902425-0-0
ISBN (ebook): 979-8-9902425-1-7

Library of Congress Control Number: 2024910385

First edition

*To the people who see a need and
reach out with loving-kindness.*

Contents

Introduction	1
Chapter 1—Twenty-Five Minutes	3
Chapter 2—The Path to My Destiny	17
Chapter 3—Taking a Different Road	24
Chapter 4—Millie	28
Chapter 5—We Have More to Contribute Than We Realize	34
Chapter 6—Creating the Vision When Obstacles Are in the Way	41
Chapter 7—When We Open Our Hearts, Lives Are Changed	53
Chapter 8—The Power of Compassion	63
Chapter 9—The Kindness of Strangers	75
Chapter 10—Hope Found	83
Chapter 11—A More Expansive Heart	94
Chapter 12—Pain Can Have a Silver Lining	102
Chapter 13—Unexpected Healing	109
Chapter 14—Turning Enthusiasm into Action	115
Chapter 15—We Are All Connected	126
Chapter 16—The Warmth of a Smile	133
Chapter 17—Sadie's North Star	139
Chapter 18—The Ripple Effect	144
Chapter 19—A Journey of Resilience and Strength	156
Chapter 20—Keeping a Promise	163
Chapter 21—An Unbroken Spirit	168
Choose to Make a Difference	175
Places Where You Are Needed	177
Citations	183
Acknowledgments	185
About the Author	187

Introduction

> There can be no greater gift than that of giving one's time and energy to help others without expecting anything in return.
>
> —Nelson Mandela

Thirty-eight years ago, I embarked on a personal mission to offer families with children experiencing homelessness a place to stay and support of various kinds to meet their needs for shelter and stabilization. My intention to be of service and to uplift people going through hard times attracted many individuals in my local community, and our success subsequently led to the creation of a nationwide movement and organization that is still going strong today. With the help of tens of thousands of volunteers, and after several evolutions in name and structure, Family Promise today serves more than 180,000 men, women, and children a year and has a strategic plan to help a million children by 2030.

As proud as I am of what has been—and will continue to be—accomplished by those who have picked up the torch from me and are running with it so capably, *Meant for More: Following Your Heart and Finding Your Purpose* at its core isn't purely about volunteering or homelessness. I would have to say I wrote this book to speak to the profound personal healing that happens when we act on our innate kindness. My instinct to show compassion to a stranger I passed on the street was guided by my heart. As a child, I experienced the terrible pain of loss, so I have always known what it's like to truly suffer and feel terribly alone, and I wouldn't want anyone else to go through similar suffering for any reason on their own. So much of the pain that is experienced in our society is preventable if only we help one another.

I wrote this book in the same spirit with which I started Family Promise all those many years ago: to initiate and spread a movement based on compassion and to raise awareness along the way of the plight of the many people who are suffering in our country because of their lack of access to social services, affordable housing, and fair wages.

As you read the stories from my life and about the lives of people who have been lifted up and who have helped others lift themselves up out of dire circumstances and misfortune, I hope that you appreciate the power of the human spirit. I hope you look into the face of another human and see yourself reflected there. The next time you have an opportunity to offer kindness to a neighbor, a friend, or a stranger on the street, I hope you listen to the impulse you feel to reach out and act on it without hesitation. And I hope you get the chance to experience the rewards of participating. Imagine what the world would look like if we all made the vow to take simple steps to build a more caring society.

Thank you for joining me on this journey of loving-kindness and your interest in hearing the stories of all the ways compassion heals us and the world.

CHAPTER 1

Twenty-Five Minutes

What we have once enjoyed we can never lose.
All that we love deeply becomes a part of us.
—Helen Keller

Nestled along the gentle coastline of Long Island Sound, Darien, Connecticut, was the backdrop to my childhood. Renowned as one of the country's most affluent areas, Darien is a harmonious blend of natural beauty mixed with opulence. It is a privileged community with five country clubs. With its charming, leafy streets lined with stunning architecture, the town is a tapestry of picturesque views. The air, infused with a subtle hint of sea salt and the soothing sounds of waves, evokes a sense of serenity that is simply irresistible. My father, Arthur Olson, was a prominent architect who designed incredibly beautiful homes, most of which were built in Darien. One of my father's creations was our charming two-story, three-bedroom home with a white picket fence on a dead-end road, making it a safe place for us children to play.

At a glance, our family appeared quite typical in this peaceful yet fun community, with its beautiful beaches and parks designed for keeping families connected and happy, especially during the summer months. There were two pretty beaches, Weed Beach and Pear Tree Point Beach. Not much else was needed to generate smiles and pure joy.

Growing up as a Presbyterian, I was obligated to attend Sunday School, and although I looked the part, I never felt like I fit in. Everyone dressed beautifully: the women wore nice dresses and white gloves, while men donned jackets and ties. The problem for me was that people seemed more concerned about appearances than God. I never saw any outreach or care for the less fortunate. Perhaps I was just picking up on the culture of the 1950s.

My innate compassion for others and for spirituality led me to seek refuge in nature, where I felt a profound connection to God. On the left side of our house, I planted daffodils that faithfully returned year after year and violets around a 4-by-6-inch perfectly heart-shaped rock with a small hole. I was unaware at the time that violets symbolize spiritual wisdom, faithfulness, and humility. Whether sitting by my rock in our flower garden in the backyard or venturing deep into the woods, climbing over the little stone wall that Native Americans built hundreds of years ago, to sit on a log with a stream running by it, the peaceful quiet of nature lifted my soul. Here, I prayed for my family and that I would endeavor to be kind to everyone.

Little did I know then that these early prayers would shape my future, leading me down a path of service and compassion for others.

The pond at the end of my street was where I made

aspirations for the future. Back then, the pond would often freeze over, allowing us to skate on it. Putting on my figure skates, I aspired to follow in the footsteps of Sonja Henie, a renowned Olympic, world, and European figure-skating champion. I spent the winter months honing my figure-skating abilities, perfecting my three-jumps and twirls in pursuit of excellence. During the summers, I reveled in carefree days spent exploring and playing with friends. We caught tadpoles and observed their transformations into frogs, built forts out of hay, and engaged in games of basketball, tag, hide-and-seek, red rover, and kick the can. These simple pleasures brought immense joy and created cherished memories.

My mother, Ruth, was an excellent swimmer. She taught me and the neighborhood kids, including my friend Dennis Holahan, how to swim and dive. On those warm sunny days, she'd pick kids up in her old four-door Chevy and take us to Pear Tree Point Beach for the day, where laughter and fun were abundant. All my friends loved her. There were swimming and diving competitions at the end of the season for children and adults. We'd watch my mother effortlessly glide through the water using perfect strokes, often winning trophies and medals for her prowess. My mother could beat practically any woman her age. Proficient at diving, she made just a little plop as she entered the water. Her legs didn't sway left or right; they were perfectly aligned. I was particularly proud of winning a trophy for "Girls 14 and Under" when I was only ten. Dennis won first place for diving year after year.

Immersing myself in the rhythmic ebb and flow of water was my greatest joy. Swimming was more than a pastime—it was a cherished bond my mother and I shared. It was a common thread that intricately wove our hearts together, transforming our relationship into an enduring tapestry of shared memories and experiences. It was, and always will be, a precious reminder of our harmonious connection. My bond with my mother was special because she saw *me*, and not only did she tell me how much she loved me, but her actions also showed her devotion, and I felt it. People need to feel acknowledged and loved. Even something as simple as her letting me lean against her shoulder while sitting on the sofa watching television together exuded love.

For the most part, I was a happy kid. But my separation anxiety from my mother caused me to cry nearly every day I was away from her when I went to school, up until the second grade. I was fortunate to have a wonderful teacher, Mrs. Struck, that second-grade year. She gave me comfort with hugs and some tools to calm myself down, like walking in the hallway and singing a little tune. I later ran into her when I was in high school, and she told me, "We teachers all have our favorites; you were mine."

When I was six, at every recess period, two boys chased me. One day, the boys chased me to the top of the jungle gym. One of the boys had an eye that went askew, which scared me. The teachers never said anything to stop them from coming after me—and at that time, girls wore dresses or skirts to school. My mother called the school to complain about this harassment, but it didn't stop. I was always exhausted when I got home. Then one day at recess, I watched, filled with a mixture of anticipation and curiosity, as my mother confidently advanced down the path toward me. I don't know what she said to those boys, but they never bothered me again.

I had a lot of good friends, but my mother was my best friend, and our good times were endless.

Naturally, I wanted that same relationship with my father, and we had moments where it seemed possible, yet, somehow, we fell short and never made a consistent connection. I thought my father worked a lot because every weekday, my neighbor's father pulled into their driveway at 5:00 p.m., which was two hours earlier than my father did, and got out of the car with his lunch pail in hand. Dad was particularly handsome, towering over everyone at six foot four, clean shaven, and well dressed. His big belly came from drinking, and his standard drink after work was a boilermaker—a shot of whiskey and a beer.

One of the good times with my father was when he taught me how to aquaplane, a board for riding on water, to cross over the wake that our 33-foot cabin cruiser, the *Heidi Ho*, made. I absolutely loved it! I had so much fun that I eventually learned how to water ski. My friend Dennis and Gaga (my mother's mother) would often come out on the boat, and Dad had friends that came, too, but they were mostly his drinking buddies. We dug for soft-shell long-neck clams, boiled them in water, and dipped them in butter. Delicious! Life, at such times, was simply beautiful.

Dad often inspected his job sites on Saturday mornings, and I tagged along with him. That and having breakfast beforehand were among my favorite things to do with him. The pancakes were always fluffy and delicious. We usually had dinner together when Dad was done working, and I enjoyed that too. People in town knew him, and I reveled in watching Dad interact with others. Besides his commanding stature, people just genuinely seemed to respect him.

Unfortunately, my father was a perfectionist, and our home life wasn't always easy. Frequently, when I was given a chore and it wasn't done to his liking, I would hear, "For God's sake, Karen, can't you do anything right?" I never felt my father liked me very much; nevertheless, anything I did with him was special to me.

My baby sister, Carol, was born when I was ten. My mother became significantly depressed after my sister's birth, and it worsened with time. I didn't know it then, but years later, I realized it was likely postpartum depression. To make matters worse, a year after Carol's birth, my mother found out my father had been having an affair with a woman from town. My parents no longer seemed like a happy, healthy couple. With their dwindling affection for one another, my mother drank her scotch and soda a little more than before. When they fought, I'd hear her repeatedly yelling, "I want out, Arthur! I want out!" I didn't know what that meant, but *out* wasn't something Dad was willing to give her. I was so worried hearing this, not knowing what I could do to help.

Pleading with my mother, Dad tried convincing her: "No! We're going to make things right, Ruth. We'll make it through this. Just hang on!"

"I want out!" she insisted, sobbing dejectedly. "I want out!" As though she was longing for something better.

By the time I was twelve, I'd look for my mother after school and find her in the kitchen, leaning over the sink. She'd lift her head, revealing red and puffy eyes, only to stare into space as though she were no longer present. The sadness blanketing her face became constant. The way she communicated was also different, alluding to the fact that she was unhappy, and since she was my best friend, I felt it too.

When people close to us change, it changes us too.

The excitement of Christmas hung in the air. I was about to leave for school. I had just turned twelve in September and was in the seventh grade. On Monday mornings, my father would take Gaga, who stayed with us on the weekends, to the station so she could catch the 7:14 a.m. train to New York City, and then she would go straight to Macy's, where she worked in the book department. After dropping Gaga off at the train station, he continued on to work.

I left at 7:35 a.m. to catch the school bus not far from home. We could almost see the bus stop from our house, a few hundred yards away and up a hill. At 8:00 a.m., Maggie, a woman who cleaned our house on Mondays, would arrive. She took the bus from one town over in Stamford, got off at a stop in Darien, and then walked to our home. Those twenty-five minutes between when I left and when Maggie came would change my life forever.

I constantly worried about my mother. The fear I had was that something would separate us, or that if I weren't with her, she'd worry about me. This wasn't really logical, but it was a lingering fear.

That morning, my mother made me buttered toast with jelly for breakfast. I ate at the kitchen table near the big bay window overlooking our backyard while she sat with me. She didn't eat. Seemingly distant, she just slowly sipped her coffee. Overhead was a jovial Santa Claus that my father painted on the window. Saint Nick, laying a finger aside his nose, with a sack full of toys, was about to climb down the chimney. My father, a talented artist, did the entire painting freehand. Who wouldn't be happy? It was that time of year!

I finished breakfast. "Come on, Carrie!" my mother said, using her nickname for me, "it's time to go to school. Don't forget your lunch box; here are your books." Then, as always, she walked me to the door—a Dutch door with windowpanes on the top half—still in her frayed, quilted pink satin bathrobe, with my baby sister balanced on her right hip. I smiled and gave her a kiss goodbye.

Usually, when I was halfway down the walk and would wave to her, she'd wave back. The next time I turned to look—and I always did—she would have left the door. This time, when I waved halfway down the walk, she waved back as expected, but when I made it to the bottom of the pathway and turned around, she was still at the door, waving. I crossed the street into the neighbor's yard, and she was still waving. I waved back. I walked through the neighbor's yard almost to the end and looked back. My mother was still waving. I waved back. I walked through the small wooded area, heading over the stone wall onto the next block, then up the hill to the bus. Again, I looked, and although I couldn't see very well through the trees, I could see our door, and I thought my mother was still waving. In case she could see me, I waved back.

The bus ride to school was relatively short, taking only ten minutes with a couple of stops. After several classes that morning, we sat at our desks to eat lunch in our homerooms because of overcrowding. My homeroom teacher, Mr. Luce, was a precise, picky guy who sometimes injected a wave of sarcasm into his teaching. Most of the kids didn't like him that much. I know I didn't, because I was somewhat afraid of him.

I sat in the third seat of the first row. I brought my lunch because I didn't care for the hot lunches in the cafeteria. However, I liked the desserts, mainly their ice-cream sandwiches, which I regularly had after finishing my sandwich.

I had eaten nearly half of the ice-cream sandwich when one of the secretaries from the principal's office, Mrs. Hall, entered the classroom. She approached Mr. Luce, who was at the front of the room, and whispered to him with her hand slightly covering her mouth. Mr. Luce looked at me, then glanced at her and nodded. She peered at me with a worried expression and left. Without changing his precise, matter-of-fact demeanor, Mr. Luce instructed, "Karen, when you finish your lunch, go to the principal's office—they need to speak with you."

Curious about why the principal needed to see me, I got up. I knew I wasn't in trouble at school, so I wasn't concerned about that; however, I worried something was wrong. Motioning for me to sit back down, Mr. Luce authoritatively instructed, "Finish your ice-cream sandwich." I respectfully sat back in my seat and gulped down the ice cream, concerned about why the principal wanted to see me.

When I entered the principal's office, I felt the secretary was visibly flustered about me or my situation. I never actually saw the principal.

"Karen, we got a call from your grandmother, and she wants you to come back home," Mrs. Hall said. "I'll drive you."

My eyes narrowed. Gaga was surely in New York City at work.

But without questioning Mrs. Hall, I climbed into the front seat of her car, sensing the ride to my house was rather uncomfortable for her. Perhaps concerned that I'd begin asking too many questions, she attempted to fill the time with light but awkward conversation.

"Do you have any brothers or sisters?"

"Yes, a sister, Carol."

"Oh, your names are very similar, Karen and Carol. Do your parents get confused when calling you by name?" she asked.

I just shook my head no. My mind was preoccupied with trying to determine why I was being taken home.

When she pulled up to our house, visibly upset yet trying to act in control, Gaga was already walking down the steps toward the car to meet me. I knew something was wrong. As calmly as possible, Gaga told me, "Mommy had a nervous breakdown, but she'll be okay." Then she added reassuringly, "She's in the hospital, and I'll stay here with you until she's better."

I'd heard the term *nervous breakdown* before, so it didn't come as a surprise. My mother had been upset for months, making it understandable that she'd had a nervous breakdown. Other people in Darien had "nervous breakdowns," so it seemed normal, something that happened to people, maybe to those who lived in the suburbs. Even so, somehow I thought things would be okay, and this was probably a phase. My mother would come out of it, and things would be better in the long run.

While my mother was always physically present, that faraway gaze suggested she was there but not really there. Her beautiful but swollen red eyes were from tears that must have been shed in my absence, because I never saw her cry, and coming home from school to find her leaning over the kitchen sink, again, with swollen eyes staring into space was a warning. I knew she was sad. And while I was often awakened at night by loud fighting between my parents, she tried to hide it from me. My father's 18-month affair with another woman was more than my mother could bear; it caused her to become heartbroken and enraged while feeling trapped at the same time. Although she loved my father, over time, my mother was worn down and exhausted.

I thought her nervous breakdown would be the wake-up call to make everything all right. But that didn't happen. Instead, I was told that since my mother was in the intensive care unit, I couldn't see her yet. When she felt better, I could visit.

The next few days were somewhat of a blur. I made a Christmas bouquet for my mother, writing on the vase, "Get Well Soon, Mommy, Love, Karen," with a note telling her not to worry about anything, that we were taking care of the baby, and for her to get better soon. I also shared that the boy I had a crush on, Steve Cram, was moving to Montana.

The following two days I stayed home from school. Neighbors came over with food, and I observed Gaga speaking in whispers, appearing frantically worried. I felt it wasn't a normal time, but as far as I was concerned, I held firmly to the belief that things would get better and that what happened to my mother was the turning point.

Sadly, I couldn't have been more wrong.

Late in the afternoon, just before dinner, I was sitting curled up on the sofa watching television. My father came into the room but didn't sit next to me or place his arm around me. Rather, he stood in front of me and said, flatly, "Mommy died."

I remember crying and screaming, "No, no, no!" as I beat my fists against my father's chest.

His only response was "Stop it! Stop it! Stop it!"

Then, he handed me a Coca-Cola with ice and two capsules and told me, "The doctor said to take this."

I must have fallen asleep or passed out quickly. It seemed

like a lifetime had passed when I finally woke up. No one told me my mother had tried to commit suicide and didn't just have a nervous breakdown, until after she died. Even when I knew the truth, I sank into a wave of denial. I didn't want to believe it. Then, I found the knife she used to slit a window screen on the second floor behind the radiator in the bathroom. She dove out the window onto her head in the backyard, breaking her neck, because she wanted out—and that was out. Those twenty-five minutes between leaving for school and Maggie finding my mother became the worst twenty-five minutes of my life.

Sympathy cards and flowers poured in while neighbors streamed in and out of our house, hugging me, crying, and grieving. Several people stopped by with containers of food, which no one seemed to eat. The reality of my mother's death hadn't sunk in. I was still wading in denial. After all, it was almost Christmas, and our tree was up. I'd given my mother my Christmas wish list—a game of Sorry and a musical jewelry box with a dancing ballerina on top that I spotted in a store. But the only thing I wanted now—was my mother.

My father didn't want me to attend the private viewing at the funeral home, because he thought it would be too much. There was some truth to his opinion, but Gaga thought I should go. I had to see my mother one last time and say goodbye. A day before the funeral, Dad took me to the viewing, and I had the privacy to see her without anyone else. Everything I felt—all of my emotions—came rushing to the surface. I burst into tears, instinctively reaching out, only to feel my father yank me back from my mother.

Three days before Christmas, I walked into Lawrence Funeral Home for my mother's funeral. I entered a room full of people dressed in black. My mother had many friends and acquaintances who came to pay their respects, but they couldn't have known the degree of pain and brokenness she'd carried. Time had only made her burden worse. My father, Gaga, other family members, and I sat placidly, holding hands in the front row. Silent through the service, I wept, tears flowing down my cheeks. The separation anxiety I'd experienced when I was away from my mother during my first few years of school was painful, yet I'd never experienced this kind of pain—the kind that could collapse my very world.

I barely heard a word the minister had to say. I just stared at the closed casket concealing my mother, fully aware that a part of me had died with her.

After my mother was buried, my father only mentioned her once, some fifteen years later when he was watching a swim meet on TV with my sister. He told Carol what a good swimmer my mother had been. Looking back, I understand now that my father's way of dealing with my mother's death was to ignore it. Back then, there weren't any grief-support programs, which I feel would have been beneficial to my family had they been available.

On Christmas Eve, my friend Dennis was given a blank Christmas card in an envelope from his mom. She told him to write a note on it to me saying, "Merry Christmas." When Dennis knocked on our door, my father answered it, while Gaga and several relatives were in the living room. Dennis told my father he had something for me and politely waited outside, since he knew why everyone was there.

I walked up to the door, and Dennis gently handed me the card and said, "Merry Christmas, Karen."

"Thank you," I said.

We didn't know how to talk about what had happened, and I didn't know how to grieve. Then, somehow, the days of my beautiful childhood memories were over. Nothing was ever the same.

Christmas came, and presents were placed under the tree, along with two unwrapped gifts. My eyes rested on the same music box I saw in the store and the game Sorry that was on my list.

CHAPTER 2

The Path to My Destiny

The meaning of life is to find your gift. The purpose of life is to give it away.

—Pablo Picasso

After my mother's passing, the world kept spinning with an unforgiving constancy that was both comforting and cruel. The sun continued to rise and set, painting the sky with colors she would no longer see. Time, in its relentless march, offered no pause for grieving hearts, and I eventually returned to school. I was thrust back into the ebb and flow of academics, navigating each day under the weight of my mother's absence.

My grandmother, Gaga, stayed with us until my father hired a housekeeper to assist with the care of my younger sister, Carol, who was two, and the upkeep of our home so we could focus on healing and moving forward. Fortunately, Dad found someone who was very loving and good to my sister. Charlotte Jones was an experienced caterer with prior housekeeping experience. She quickly proved to be an excellent caregiver for my sister, treating her with love and care as if she were her own daughter. Though it was beautiful to observe Charlotte's interactions with Carol, mine with her were limited. It wasn't that I didn't want a relationship with Charlotte; it was that we weren't authentically close. Aside from keeping the house, cooking, and doing laundry, she spent nearly all her time with my sister. Charlotte and Carol had dinner around 4:30 or 5:00 p.m. I would wait for my father to come home before eating, but most nights I ate alone because my father was out drinking.

Feeling incredibly lonely and longing for the comfort my mother had provided, I mustered up the courage to ask Charlotte if I could join her while she watched TV in her room. I wanted only a sliver of the love and comfort she generously gave Carol. She left the room and returned with a straight-back chair, placing it off to the side where I could still see the television, but she didn't allow me to be in a position to receive the same warmth and love she gave my sister.

"Can I just lie on your bed?" I asked.

"No," she snapped.

Concealing the pain that threatened to surface, I dropped my head and asked in a whisper barely louder than a heartbeat, "Why can't I?"

"I don't want someone wallowing in my bed," she replied sharply.

Feeling such a stark difference from what I'd had with my mother was hurtful. Leaving Charlotte's room, feeling discarded and completely unwanted, I wandered into the living room, sat on the couch, propped my head up on a pillow, and watched *The Honeymooners*, a show my mother and I had enjoyed together.

Knowing now that nothing could fill the profound void

my mother had left, I found comfort in immersing myself in the routine of school and time with friends. But when night fell, I suffered through the silence, and I'd cry myself to sleep, hugging Mike the Cat, a stuffed toy that Mike, one of my father's friends, had given me. It had a rubber smiley face that my incessant tears washed away within a few short months. It had become my companion, confidant, and friend.

My bed was near two sizable paned glass windows, and at night I'd look out at the stars and the moon into a future I hoped would be better. The deep, wrenching pain was so unbearable that I could only pray, "God, bless Mommy and keep her safe, and may she be happy. Oh please, dear God, help me to love everyone. Oh God, please help me make sense of all this."

With my mother gone, my father, Carol, and I had adjustments to make. I treated Carol like my baby, and Gaga, a bit eccentric but like a mother, became my lifeline. She still came to our house on the weekends until my father recommended I go to New York to see her instead. At twelve years old, I jumped at the chance to take the forty-five-minute train to Grand Central Station to see Gaga. When I rode the subway from Grand Central Station to Macy's, I'd walk up West 34th Street and stroll into the entrance of 151 Macy's. While Gaga worked in the book department, I'd wander the nine floors of the magnificent department store, fantasizing about dresses, furniture, linens, China sets, glassware, toys, and practically everything else. It would take hours to explore all the floors. New York was simply another world, and I thought it incredibly exciting to see all the glitz of the big city. By comparison, I deemed Darien homogenous and stifling. The sameness became boring, and with my mother no longer there, I felt boxed in. But with all its lights and the symphony of sounds assembled in its streets, New York City was a potpourri of diversity at its finest. It represented the real world with people of different colors, races, and cultures. I loved it!

I couldn't wait to meet Gaga on her break, and we'd usually have lunch with a couple of her friends, Tony and Freddie, across the street at Astor Cafeteria. Afterward, Gaga would return to work, and I would continue to explore the various floors in Macy's. When Gaga's workday was over, we'd meet up and head uptown to her apartment. We would take the subway to 110th Street and Broadway. Keeping a comfortable pace with Gaga, I learned to dodge the swarms of people filling the sidewalk.

During one of these visits with my grandmother, I saw a man in his seventies on my grandmother's block who I assumed was homeless. Hunched over on the street wearing a rimmed, beaten-up hat; a ratted gray coat buttoned with an assortment of silver safety pins; and a pair of oversize, tattered brown shoes falling off his feet, he pulled at my heartstrings.

When my eyes rested upon him, I felt a wave of natural compassion for the elderly man, and I told Gaga, "Let's get him something to eat and maybe some gloves. Let's help him."

Instead, Gaga tugged at my hand, leading me away as we strolled past him, explaining, "He's a bum. Sometimes people like that want to be that way, but they may have thousands of dollars tucked in their bags," she whispered, turning my empathy into fear.

He was carrying two bags, tightly clutched in each hand as if they were valuable. It was stark how the man took twelve steps on 112th Street toward Broadway, put his bags down, and turned to face the Cathedral of St. John the Divine, one of the largest churches in the world. It was then that he gracefully lifted his hands to his face in prayer, mumbling something. Then, rather routinely, he picked up his two bags only to repeat his ritualistic behavior. He may have been a very religious man, but I sensed that, in some way, he was suffering, or perhaps hurting from hunger or loneliness. I knew what pain felt like, and I knew that *he* was carrying something heartbreaking with him. It seemed as though I'd become adept at sensing pain.

Gaga taught me to light a candle for those who had passed. Since she lived right across from the Cathedral of St. John the Divine, I'd go there on weekends to pray and light a candle for my mother. Being in the cathedral, abounding in hope as if I were closer to God, temporarily removed me from a hurting world.

When I was entering eighth grade, my father wanted me to go to Rosemary Hall, a prestigious girls' school in Greenwich, Connecticut, and board there. I had an interview with the dean, who settled in her high-back leather chair and asked me a bunch of questions. Feeling comfortable with my father not in the room, I didn't hold back in my responses, rattling off my interpretation of the reasons my father wanted me in boarding school, not excluding his affair and my general dislike of the idea of leaving home. Scribbling a few notes on a tablet, she listened intently, taking it all in. Then, electing a rather direct approach with my father, the dean spoke with him, firmly recommending, "Karen doesn't want to be here, and I think she belongs at home."

And my father took me home.

Two years after my mother's death, when Carol was four and I was fourteen, my father remarried a woman with two children. We moved into the house we were originally supposed to move into with my mother—one of the beautiful homes my father built. The pain of my mother's death followed me there, resonating deeply for some time.

I felt I needed to reach beyond the place I had settled and try to give others what they needed. The natural response for me was to display empathy and compassion for others who had suffered a loss or endured a painful or adverse situation, and became a reminder of who I was as a person and that I had something to offer.

I applied to the local hospital to be a candy striper. Although there were different jobs for candy stripers, I asked to deliver flowers because it seemed to be the thing that made patients in the hospital happy or at least gave them a fleeting smile. And if they were feeling down or lonely, I wanted them to feel like they could talk to me when I entered their room to deliver a gift from someone who'd thought about them. I didn't foresee that each display of kindness would nurture my compassion for others while providing something I needed. I couldn't save my mother and didn't understand the layers of her internal suffering. However, it became instinctive to acknowledge what others needed, show compassion, and continue to find ways to impact lives.

After what happened to my mother, her loss helped me identify more clearly that I wanted—or needed—to help people, and I found that serving others was the way. A teenage boy who lived across the street from us was dying of cancer. Whenever I saw him, looking jaundice and so thin, I could sense that whatever joy he'd had dissipated because of the cancer. You could see the sadness in his eyes. Feeling he needed the warmth and happiness that kindness can bring, I played tennis with him, talked to him, and prayed for him, knowing I couldn't change his outcome but hoping I could make his days a little brighter.

Whether or not I knew it at the time, I was following the path of my destiny. It wouldn't be an easy path; nevertheless, it was mine to take.

CHAPTER 3

Taking a Different Road

> Your present circumstances don't determine where you can go; they merely determine where you start.
>
> —Nido Qubein

Nobody's life is ever a straight path, and where we set off to go might not be where we end up. I didn't know where my life would lead, but it was destined to be something unimaginable. During high school, I knew I wanted to do something that would make a difference in the lives of others, so I decided to become a nurse. Fiercely motivated, I worked hard and studied, achieving As in biology and chemistry, because they were the prerequisites for nursing school, while getting Bs and Cs in my other classes. My stepmother, never one to shy away from making her thoughts known, told me, "I was a nurse. You'll *never* be a nurse. You don't have the grades for it."

Crushed when my father and stepmother shut the door on my decision to attend nursing school, I made a hard pivot.

I studied hard and acquired an associate's degree in business administration, which set me on a slightly different path. I was confident that something ahead of me would allow me to serve others, regardless of the field. I was wired to help others.

At twenty-two, I became an assistant to one of the many vice presidents of an advertising agency, SSC&B, in New York City. Whenever I left in the evening, a handsome young man was always seated behind the front desk. Several girls working there had already noticed him. Larry introduced himself and said he was the night watchman while he was getting his MBA at Columbia during the day.

Years earlier, when I was fourteen, I had chosen to take an art class as an elective in school. Initially, I used the time in class to socialize and fool around with my friends. After seeing a lovely Joseph Turner painting of Venice from 1835 and remembering how much my grandmother loved Venice, I was inspired by my love for Gaga to paint a replica of it for her. It was then I realized I loved drawing and painting and had the gift to paint.

Painting was cathartic. Immersion in colors, creativity, and silence filled me with a sense of internal peace and calmness. One afternoon while I was still working at SSC&B, I took my paints to the Columbia University campus, where I sat to paint a tree. I saw Larry as he crossed the lawn, heading in my direction. He came over, said hello, and after talking a little bit, asked me out to dinner. We spent time getting to know one another, and what I liked about him was his kindness and his sense of humor.

After a few months, when I was just twenty-two, he asked me to marry him. I said yes. I had a strong desire to restore some sense of a home and family of my own.

Shortly after we married, Larry took a position with Procter & Gamble, relocating us to Cincinnati, Ohio, where we had our first child, Brad. While Cincinnati was a wonderful place to raise a family, I was incredibly close with my sister, Carol, who was fourteen years old then. I couldn't help but think of the many times I'd taken her to New York when she was a little girl. I'd hold her hand, and she would jump up and down when I squeezed it. Whenever we got together when we were older, we had fun, giggling for no reason other than being in each other's company. I missed Carol, Gaga, and my father. Luckily, four years later, Larry got a job at Johnson & Johnson, and we moved to East Windsor, New Jersey, placing me closer to my family in Connecticut. And there, we had our second child, Doug. Although I was thrilled to be a mom for a second time, I suffered bouts of depression, which I later learned was postpartum depression.

I often wondered how lonely my mother must have been to take her life, which turned the many wonderful memories I had of my early childhood into somewhat of a difficult holiday season or reflection on my past. Rather than sit in my pain, I felt compelled to do something for someone who might be alone. I never knew exactly what that would be, but giving of myself brought a sense of healing. I felt if others had acknowledged my mother when she was alive, been kinder in trying to understand what she'd been going through, and given her the opportunity to express herself without judgment, it might have been the difference between hopeless and hopeful, or life and death. Regardless of my trials and tribulations, knowing that we all have them, my focus was better served by extending my hand to others. I believe we've all had difficult times, and kindness could have been the cure. Because I'd experienced tremendous suffering in my childhood, I knew what it was like to deal with grief, agony, depression, and loss. I innately cared about others and wanted to bring them solace.

—

Unfortunately, my marriage to Larry didn't last beyond seven years for several reasons, and we went our separate ways. He moved to New York City but came back to New Jersey on weekends to visit with the boys. We got along well, and Larry was always supportive. After our divorce, the weight of being a single mother brought on feelings of anxiety and depression that continued for several years. Thankfully, I was treated for this and was in a good place to go back to work. Over the course of the next seven years, my career opportunities expanded, starting with a job at Webcraft Printing Company. I clearly had an aptitude for business and was made an assistant to a sales manager. Don Jagoda Associates, a promotional agency, was a client of Webcraft's, and they offered me a job as an account executive. One of the companies I was in charge of was Warner-Lambert, a pharmaceutical company where I later worked. I was a promotion manager responsible for Schick razors and Listerine.

CHAPTER 4

Millie

> Too often we underestimate the power of a touch, a smile, a kind word, a listening ear, an honest compliment, or the smallest act of caring, all of which have the potential to turn a life around.
>
> —Leo F. Buscaglia

During the years after my divorce, I traveled to New York City frequently for meetings. New York has always been one of my favorite places, and it has always been magnificently decorated during the holidays. Yet, despite the cheery facade, plight and pain were hiding in plain sight. I had long observed my surroundings and the people in it, and I couldn't help but notice people who were sitting or lying over a subway grate, in doorways, or stretching out a hand to ask for money. It was difficult to walk a city block without seeing someone who was obviously homeless. Like many other passersby, although I saw them, I would look away and walk straight past. Though I never said anything to these people, my spirit told me it wasn't right.

Then one particular day in November 1981, fate intervened. I was on my way to a business meeting on Lexington Avenue when my eyes rested on a withered, homeless woman wearing a cap over her gray hair, appearing to be in her seventies. She was perched on a worn crate in front of the bustling Grand Central Station, two weather-beaten bags brimming with her life's possessions were nestled at her side. I had seen her before—her rounded shoulders sagging under an invisible weight, and her eyes, dull and desolate, gazing down at the unforgiving pavement as though the prospect of lifting her eyes to the horizon was a luxury too far beyond her grasp. Her posture evoked her sense of despair, a poignant testament to having forsaken all hope.

That day, I couldn't just walk past her without doing or saying something. Quite impulsively, I darted across the street into a store and bought the woman a ham-and-cheese sandwich with orange juice. When I handed it to her, she lifted her head and, in a heartfelt whisper, said, "Thank you. God bless you. I haven't eaten anything since yesterday." She tentatively extended her hand toward me, and as I enveloped her rough, calloused hand with my own, I was struck by the warmth emanating in this touch, a testimony to a heart that had held on to love amid so much adversity. It was in this intimate exchange that it felt like an indelible spiritual bond was forged between us. This moment marked my crossing over an unseen threshold, a shift in perspective that would irrevocably alter my understanding of humanity and kinship.

An air of urgency seemed to envelop her as if she wished for me to depart her side with an understanding of her narrative securely etched in my memory.

She told me her name was Millie. I was compelled to listen, notably when she told me that the toughest part of her life was feeling invisible among the swarms of people walking by. Millie told me a little about her life, that she had been married and that her husband was a chef. Unfortunately, he had a heart attack and died. She had no savings or insurance to fall back on and had lost her single-occupancy apartment when it was renovated into condominiums. Millie spent some nights in a shelter, but the women's shelters were difficult to get into. Occasionally, she slept in Grand Central Station, but they would kick her out at a specific time, so with nowhere to go, she never knew where she could call home. Millie wasn't a homeless woman; she was a human being experiencing homelessness, a widow, and a mother of two sons. One of her sons lived on the West Coast, and the other had died. With her diminished self-worth, she sat in silence, disconnected from humanity in her own cold world. I knew experiencing homelessness wasn't the way for anyone to live out their life.

Before leaving her side, I leaned toward her and said, reassuringly, "You'll get by." Then, choking up, I, too, had to walk away and rush to my meeting, without knowing where her next meal would come from, if not for an act of kindness from a stranger. I wondered if I could have done more. It was humbling to discover that the smallest act of kindness for Millie would take me across the line, breaking a barrier that enabled me to reach more of the population who were experiencing homelessness.

Until then, I didn't think we should approach homeless people, partly because of what Gaga taught me and somewhat due to the stigma associated with the homeless population, a common conception that they were on drugs or caught up in alcoholism, violence, or mental illness. But now I was getting involved, and I learned a simple yet invaluable equation: when we take the time to honor and dignify the humanity in others, notably the most vulnerable among us, our own humanity begins to shine like never before.

Before meeting Millie, I assumed that someone else would see the individuals in need, struggling on the street, and help them. Millie's response to me let me know that I could help, and that my help was what she needed. Though I had struggled with depression, just as I had endured difficult times at various points in my life, I realized people can get into a rut and need help. It may take a little effort, but I began to understand that people like Millie needed help to get back on their feet.

I began to see that the practice of being present to what is around me enabled me to perceive reality with greater clarity, fostering an even deeper sense of empathy as I became attuned to the experiences of others. This kind of empathic understanding allows us to transcend superficial judgments, acknowledging the nuanced and often inescapable factors that precipitate certain life situations. I began awakening to the truer narrative behind what causes someone to lose their home. There are circumstances, some predictable and others unforeseen, that remain out of people's control, such as a fire. A death. Health issues. Job loss. Mental illness. Then, there are reasons like financial instability, substance abuse, physical or sexual abuse, and a host of other multilayered challenges that can lead to individuals and families becoming homeless.

Learning to see those who are going through a hard time as people just like you or me was the beginning of my journey.

The lines had blurred for me, and I looked at the world in two ways. Originally, I believed we shouldn't go near these people living on the streets, especially if we have children with us. Then I looked at the situation another way and thought, Of course, we should! These are God's children, and the need is there. Embracing the alternate, more inclusive view of the world removed my fear and compelled me to take action.

After meeting Millie, I returned home and told Brad, twelve, and Doug, ten, about her. Intrigued and eager to help, Doug said, "Mom, let's go to New York and find more people like Millie," and so we did. The act of doing something for those overlooked felt necessary. That one small act of kindness to Millie was contagious, and I realized I could do more—much more. After making twenty-five ham-and-cheese, roast-beef, and turkey deli sandwiches and amassing some granola bars, my sons and I filled our backpacks and headed to New York. Rollerblading through Central Park, we handed out sandwiches and snack bars without knowing how great the need was.

The next time we ventured to New York City, we went to the Port Authority Bus Terminal. We saw more people like Millie gathered or sleeping on benches, and we wanted to give them sandwiches too. We made forty sandwiches that time, and our stash was quickly depleted. We resolved to bring even more the next time, and with each subsequent visit, we increased our deliveries, making as many as one hundred sandwiches. The sandwich was a vehicle to say we cared. Wherever we went, we saw the need.

We handed out sandwiches and granola bars and struck up conversations. Some recipients were suspicious of us, so we left food nearby so they could find it for themselves without feeling like they were getting handouts. The food was certainly welcome, but what seemed more meaningful to the people we met was that we were willing to stop and talk to them, and we weren't afraid of them simply because they were homeless. And over time, people waited for us on the benches we routinely visited.

"We hoped we'd see you," they'd say. "How are you?" After that, it was mostly just small talk, but we learned that kindness made a difference, whether it was through a smile, a handshake, a meal, a coat, a blanket, or whatever we could offer. Following my heart's impulse was proving to be helpful to others—it was vital.

Millie's sadness and loneliness had been so profound that it moved me to look for her every time I went into the city and passed by Grand Central Station. I always hoped she was okay. Millie was a gift to me—divine intervention—setting me on the path to taking action. God put us in touch with one another, and though I never saw her again, that encounter with Millie changed my life. It made me realize that when we take the time to dignify and honor the humanity in others, we bring out the best in ourselves and those around us. It is a simple yet invaluable equation that reminds us of our interconnectedness and the power of small acts of kindness to change the world.

CHAPTER 5

We Have More to Contribute Than We Realize

> Never think what you have to offer is insignificant. There will always be someone out there that needs what you have to give.
>
> —Anonymous

We often feel conflicted when a homeless person approaches us. Though we may be willing to give some change or even a few dollars for a meal, we second-guess ourselves and wonder if they will use the money to buy alcohol or drugs. When we see a young person begging, we ask ourselves, "Why can't they get a job?" We hesitate, feeling uncomfortable about giving or not giving them something, and these mixed feelings come to the fore every time we hear the word *homeless*. Unfortunately, the stereotyped perceptions of what homelessness is in our society are reinforced by how people experiencing homelessness are portrayed in the programs we watch on television and in films. Many people who are visible members of our communities, working alongside us and in the businesses we frequent, can be homeless without us recognizing them as people in need of a place to live that they can afford.

The "homeless" are not a single population with the same issues but rather a diverse group of people with unique circumstances that have led them to their current situation. Some of those unseen as experiencing homelessness are families, children, veterans, young people aging out of the foster care system, the unemployed, and the underemployed.

Every other Sunday for two years after I gave a sandwich to Millie, my children and I made trips to the city to hand out sandwiches to the homeless. The homeless were people facing hardships, and some were hurting like I had in the past, suffering in silence. My children and I knew we should stop and help if we could. When we got to know people individually, we invited some back home for Thanksgiving dinner on several occasions. I would go into the city a few weeks in advance and deliver a bus ticket for those invited. They'd arrive in our well-to-do suburb by bus, looking conspicuous and vulnerable in their ragged clothes. Watching them shambling up our manicured front path, I could understand why some of my neighbors might have thought I was crazy, but I always believed that my community extended beyond my family and neighborhood.

Believing we are all connected, these experiences revealed something greater. Something was tugging at me to the point where I began to feel a sense of responsibility to help people experiencing homelessness, but I needed to understand why this demographic existed in the wealthiest country on Earth.

Close to Christmas, my children and I ventured into the city to deliver new little gifts, like gloves, hats, and socks, to those in need. But more importantly, we invested in getting to know them, discovering that they seemed to value being wished a merry Christmas with a warm hug more than gifts.

For several years, my sons and I celebrated three different Christmases. The first was in Summit, New Jersey, when their father would join us on Christmas morning. It didn't take much to pause and realize how blessed we were with the abundance of presents under the tree—admittedly, more than anyone needed. Later that day, we had a wonderful Christmas dinner with my father and sister in Darien, Connecticut, followed by more thoughtful gifts. But the real Christmas occurred between the two, when we stopped at the Port Authority Bus Terminal and Grand Central Station on our way to Connecticut, laden with gifts wrapped in Christmas paper with bows and gift tags that said, "Merry Christmas!" Our gifts were given from the heart and were noticeably received the same way.

"God bless you. Is this for me? Thank you," the recipients would reply appreciatively, offering a hug and receiving our warmth in return. Despite their circumstances, and although it was a small gesture, we never knew how it would impact someone. It filled my heart with joy, knowing we had made somebody's day brighter. Maybe we gave someone just enough hope, enabling them to hang on longer and believe things would improve. Given how difficult Christmas had been for me after my mother died, our actions reminded me of its true meaning.

A number of months later, on a freezing day in New York City, I was about to pass a woman sitting on the sidewalk on the corner of Sixth Avenue and 56th Street who was shivering in a thin sweater, and I stopped to talk to her. Since she didn't have a coat, I took mine off and insisted, "Here, take my coat."

"No," she replied. Genuinely concerned for me, she added, "Then *you* won't have one."

"Well, then I'll buy one," I replied, trying to ease her concerns.

I went into a nearby store and bought a coat to show the woman I wouldn't be without one, then returned, handing her the new one. Exuding humility and genuine gratitude, she slipped the coat on and buttoned it, thanking me profusely. When I continued on my way, I did so knowing she would be a little warmer. Instinctively, I knew when something was the right thing to do—and kindness always seemed right to me.

The Port Authority removed many of the benches in the bus terminal because many homeless people gathered and slept on them. The benches that remained were modified with seat dividers that made it impossible to lie down. However, with nowhere else to go, especially during the winter, they kept making the terminal their home, and we continued going there to find them. We met an elderly woman, Lucille, who lived under an escalator with her little black-and-white kitten in her bag. It had the softest fur and stunning emerald eyes. It became apparent that Lucille loved her kitten more than she did herself. At first, she was shy and quiet, but eventually she opened up and talked more. Lucille told us she was Jewish, once a first-grade teacher, and a loner who kept to herself. Although she was disheveled in appearance, she donned a fashionable hat accessorized with necklaces and pins as if she were going out on the town, vestiges of dignity from her past. I could see she was a lady embarrassed by her situation.

Lucille was pleasant and willing to talk with us on her good days. "It's so nice to see you," she'd begin. And then Lucille would speak about the weather, noticed if I had changed my hair, asked how I was doing, and made small talk like everything was normal. She even asked if I had a man friend or a new beau. Then she'd turn and chat with my sons, Brad and Doug, about their schoolwork and friends.

"You study hard, Doug! You don't want to end up like me," she'd warn, when she was on her medication. But when she was off it, Lucille had delusions, thinking that we were from the FBI and simultaneously claiming the CIA was after her too. It was impossible to calm her paranoia on those days, so we left Lucille alone then. I knew she was appreciative that we came every other Sunday.

I used caution when doing what I thought was right, but it wasn't long before I realized that interacting with most homeless people wasn't a risk. These were just people who needed something to eat and someone to talk to once in a while. They didn't present any danger to my boys. But I will say that my adventures among the homeless at the Port Authority with Brad and Doug garnered numerous reactions from commuters.

Indeed, many people thought something was wrong with me delivering sandwiches in New York, especially since I had my sons with me. They'd ask, "Aren't you afraid?" This helped me to understand that fear was the biggest obstacle when reaching out to those who are down on their luck. It's not that people don't want to help—they're afraid. This is partly because the places where the homeless congregate are not places they would typically go, and perhaps they appear threatening. Sometimes the homeless have mental and emotional problems that make people afraid of what they might physically do when they're shouting or sounding aggressive.

Not only did I feel safe interacting with and helping people living on the streets, but I came to learn that people living on the streets are the ones who are most at risk—sleeping out in the open makes the homeless more vulnerable and far more likely to be attacked or robbed. Some of the people sleeping in the Port Authority basement would tell us how they'd wake up in the morning to find that their pockets had been slit open in the night and that what little money they might have been holding on to had been stolen.

Even so, I understood people's hesitations to interact with those who are homeless, and simply gathered that there weren't many among the more fortunate who were willing to venture as far out of their comfort zone. Given these fears, I had no idea whether I could persuade anyone else to help, but my instincts told me I had to at least try—and it worked in so many wonderful ways.

When Lucille's little kitten died, she was devastated and, sad to say, truly alone. I'd told my mailman Ron Gonzalez about Lucille, and he so thoughtfully bought her another one to love so she wouldn't feel the weight of loneliness. It was beautiful to see that some who knew what we were doing wanted to help.

A friend of mine, Bob Nielsen, often joined us on our sandwich runs. He got to know a homeless man named John who had an amputated leg. He'd take John first, and then Arthur, a gentleman and World War II veteran who wore his medals inside his jacket, back to his house for a warm shower, dinner, and a safe place to sleep. John felt respected, cared for, and no longer alone. Almost every Sunday, Bob would drive back to New York to see him, find a parking spot, and let him sleep in his car. When he opened his door, he was really opening his heart. This is how change happens. I saw more good people in the world and those willing to do good—such as Bob and his wife, Anita.

Theologian Pierre Teilhard de Chardin said, "We are not human beings having a spiritual experience. We are spiritual beings having a human experience." I identified more with my spirit, which helped me cross the line into helping.

My journey showed me that people effect change through the care and concern shown to the human beings forgotten by society, giving hope to the hopeless and engaging in interactions that forever impact us. The love and compassion I felt didn't allow fear to bubble up as a deterrent; I refused to let it in. My purpose and faith were greater than fear.

CHAPTER 6

Creating the Vision When Obstacles Are in the Way

> Obstacles don't have to stop you. If you run into a wall, don't turn around and give up. Figure out how to climb it, go through it, or work around it.
>
> —Michael Jordan

The term *homeless* invariably brings to mind the depiction of a disheveled older man sleeping on a subway grate or a cardboard box under a bridge abutment with a bottle of alcohol next to him, or it evokes similar images, as well as feelings and judgments. It is easy to recognize that men and women in such a condition may suffer from addiction or mental illness. But this image is only the most visible of the homeless. You may have seen a homeless mother with a baby in her arms or pushing a stroller, and she went unnoticed by you because she didn't fit the stereotype. The issue of homelessness, particularly involving families, often remains obscured from public view, rendering these families essentially invisible within our society.

After I had been delivering sandwiches in Port Authority for a couple of years, a friend challenged me to look for where homelessness existed in my own community. As I dug into the facts, I discovered, to my dismay, that families with children represented the most rapidly expanding demographic within the homeless population, constituting approximately 35 percent of its ranks—a stark and tragic reality in a nation as prosperous as ours. I learned there were many families that were homeless and yet most of us had no idea. Spurred by this knowledge, I became steadfast in my resolve to assist these families without homes.

I had worked in corporate marketing for seven years, including four years for the pharmaceutical company Warner-Lambert and three as a consultant. In 1984, I decided to resign so I could get more involved in volunteering, which led me to focus more on finding solutions to help families experiencing homelessness. Soon after, I started volunteering at a soup kitchen in Elizabeth, New Jersey, where I met homeless families.

I began to learn that homelessness has no boundaries. It is indiscriminate and affects every community across the country. There were many homeless families in my county and across the country, and yet most of us had no idea. Why not, I asked? Because they were mainly out of sight, sleeping in cars, doubling up with relatives, bunking with friends, or even staying in campgrounds.

You and I know homeless families, even if we are unaware of their circumstances. The young woman who takes our burger order at lunch or who works as a cashier in a neighborhood store may live in her car behind the store. All we see is a girl with a smile, telling us to "Have a good day." But after her shift, she returns to her car, where she lives with her children, which is packed with what little belongings they have left after an eviction or that they could fit in the vehicle. From a Legal Aid attorney, I learned that in Union County, New Jersey at the time, the primary reason kids were being taken from their parents and placed in foster care wasn't abuse or neglect; it was homelessness. If they couldn't put a roof over their heads, the courts deemed them unfit. The harsh reality of these families' experiences opened my eyes.

Before long, a mission began to form inside me. I wanted to find ways to provide safe shelter to the homeless families in my community. But even more, I wanted to do so in a way that restored their dignity, acknowledged their humanity, and gave them a true feeling of home—a task of equal, if not greater, importance.

With the assistance of two generous angels, a surprising pair of fortuitous occurrences enabled me to dedicate my full attention to helping homeless families, making it possible for me to launch an organization. First, my father bought me a beautiful house. Second, Morris Bolsky, a respected friend with a strong sense of social justice, began to help me prepare proposals and communications. Later, without prompting, Morris underwrote my vision by providing financial support equivalent to a salary. Over time, after seeing the growth of the group across the nation, he said, "This is the best investment I ever made."

Before I took up the cause for homeless families, I had no expectation of becoming a leader. I'd done presentations at my office, but I was not a seasoned public speaker or a fundraiser. My passion for helping people instilled in me the drive to achieve my vision. That is what enabled me to assume a leadership role. At some point, I decided to act as if anything was possible.

Not everyone reacted as though we were doing something out of the ordinary when I told them about my mission to help homeless families, and a few individuals even asked to join in. For example, when I invited a group of homeless people from New York over for Thanksgiving, Bill Harrison, a neighbor, volunteered to cook the turkey. Another neighbor, Jane Fleming, heard what I was doing and offered to prepare all the side dishes. Compassion is contagious!

I assumed the religious congregations in Elizabeth would immediately want to get involved in sheltering families in need, but initially my suggestion was met with hesitation. Several said, "We're already helping the homeless. They come into our churches at night and sleep in our pews. Half of our congregations are homeless or at risk of being homeless." The pastors of area churches felt like they were already doing everything they could.

Acknowledging their existing commitments, I pivoted. It occurred to me that the first step was to bring awareness to the plight of homeless families. Awareness is the precursor to empathy and involvement. People move to the suburbs for a myriad of reasons, including to feel safe and to get away from problems traditionally associated with poverty, like homelessness. I needed to convince members of congregations in other towns, most of whom had a secure home, family, or support network, that the people we wanted to help were like them but had fallen on hard times. My instincts encouraged me to be persistent.

In 1985, I orchestrated an all-day conference on family homelessness, "You Can Make a Difference," designed to educate attendees about homeless families and the issues they face. In preparation, I created professional-looking flyers and posters, then took them to as many churches and synagogues as I could find in Union County. I handed them out, knocked on doors, and spoke with countless people, talking up a storm. For the conference sponsor, I listed the Interfaith Council for the Homeless of Union County, although this council didn't officially exist! My sons, Brad and Doug; my friends Bob and Anita Nielsen; and I were it.

Brad and Doug, who were always by my side, helped in the parking lot, directing traffic. Bob and Anita prepared sandwiches. Due to the genuine interest I'd seen, I was confident we'd have at least a hundred attendees. Admission cost only $5. But when we saw the turnout, Bob exclaimed, "Karen, you have two hundred people out there!" My perseverance and instincts had paid off! We'd proved that people did have compassion and wanted to make a difference.

Bob was wonderfully supportive, giving me hugs and telling me how great I was doing while teasing me about the workload I had placed on their shoulders. "What are you making us do?" he joked. But without faltering, he and Anita made more sandwiches.

Another friend of mine, Bob Hayes, a Wall Street attorney, gave the keynote address. Significantly impacted by all the homeless people he encountered in downtown Manhattan, Bob had filed a class-action litigation, *Callahan v. Carey*, asserting the legal right to shelter. A landmark victory in 1979 established a right to shelter for homeless men in New York. Unfortunately, Robert Callahan, the homeless man Bob had been fighting for, died on the city's streets before the consent decree was signed in December of that same year. Bob then founded the Coalition for the Homeless. In 1983, a right to shelter for homeless women was added.

Genuinely wanting the conference to be interfaith, I invited a rabbi, a minister, and a priest to facilitate. Wendy, a courageous mother who experienced homelessness, inspired attendees when she shared her story from the stage about staying at a shelter with her son while pregnant. "Each morning," she said, "the staff would say, 'Goodbye and God bless you,' and I'd have to walk around all day without knowing if we would have a bed that night when we returned to the shelter." But her story didn't end there. Wendy went on to tell us that she eventually gave birth prematurely to another son, who died due to complications.

Hearing Wendy's story introduced people from the suburbs to a different type of homeless person, someone they could have helped had they known about her plight.

After Wendy spoke, I took a moment to educate the audience about the tens of thousands of people like Wendy and the escalating statistics. "If we work together, people like Wendy will have a home," I assured them. Assessing the room, I then asked, "We're going to have a follow-up meeting in two weeks at Christ Church in Summit; how many of you are willing to attend?"

I didn't want the conference just to be educational. I wanted to ensure that action would be taken. When I scanned the room, virtually every hand went up, indicating that now that people were aware, they cared. I didn't know exactly where we were going yet, but it was clear the direction was forward. After the conference, we did in fact hold our first planning meeting at Christ Church in Summit, New Jersey, where thirty people showed up. We discussed different ways to help the homeless. Some suggestions were assembling care baskets, donating clothing, and creating a soup kitchen, but the obvious pressing need was for a shelter. There were only two shelters in Union County at the time, and these were usually filled to capacity with only one-quarter of the beds allocated to families.

Following the meeting, we began looking for a suitable building to be used as a shelter, but we were met with obstacles like zoning issues and people who didn't want a shelter in their neighborhood. When we couldn't find a building and saw that no individual church had the capacity to become a full-time shelter, we had to get creative. What if the religious communities banded together? I recommended we get a dozen or so congregations to commit to an arrangement where they would shelter families on a weekly rotational basis. That way, any one congregation would serve as a shelter only once a quarter, and it would not be a burdensome responsibility. This idea garnered enthusiasm. From there, the faithful individuals coming to the meetings were one of the ways I recruited congregations; they helped get theirs on board.

Hospitality is a virtue all faiths hold in common, so I named the organization the Interfaith Hospitality Network (IHN). I wanted to mobilize the resources of all faiths and the civic community and allow them an opportunity to work together to offer shelter and support services for homeless families. The word *interfaith* would draw from congregations of all faiths rather than one. Although I quickly found that collaborating across denominational and religious divides did not come naturally to congregations, the caveat was that I presented an opportunity for this unfamiliar style of collaboration to happen meaningfully.

The word *hospitality* denoted that this program would show respect for families and the potential for relationships between guests and volunteers to evolve organically. Guests and hosts would come together and get to know one another. And the word *network* referenced how we would draw upon the support of many community agencies and resources.

I poured myself into building the Interfaith Hospitality Network. I'd sit alone at my dining room table with piles of index cards with names of contacts stacked in front of me while going through them and making phone calls. I started contacting clergy and scheduling appointments to ask them to host homeless families in their buildings and to become a host congregation. I was genuinely enthusiastic and devoted to the cause. People were looking to me to make it happen, and I could only rise to the challenge. Along the way, I encouraged others to join me, and many did.

Perseverance was needed as I encountered skeptics. Early on, another faction involved in the IHN insisted my plan would never fly, stating, "Congregations will never allow homeless people through their doors." So, although I was moving forward, it felt like a constant undertow was dragging me backward.

Overall, my proposed program was met with enthusiasm in Union County; however, there was resistance from certain members of my board who advocated for a fundraising-only model, as opposed to providing direct service. They aimed to raise funds from affluent individuals and to subsequently donate those funds to other organizations. After a few contentious board meetings, I couldn't help but cry in my car on the way home, not understanding why these people couldn't see that we could directly help families. Despite my frustration, I was undeterred. Each roadblock in my path made me even more determined to proceed.

Interestingly, one board member, a pastor, volunteered to fine-tune our bylaws, but his revisions changed our operational focus solely to fundraising. Recognizing the implications of this change, I approached an attorney in the pastor's congregation and discussed the need to revert the bylaws. He said, "Don't worry, I will handle it. The bylaws will be changed for approval at the next meeting." True to his word, he did.

Although there was opposition, my strong conviction to house homeless families never allowed me to quit. Isabel Devenney, a former first-grade teacher in her late seventies, attended the inaugural conference. She was a stalwart member of Christ Church and generously offered us the use of Lyle Hall at Christ Church for our meetings. She'd sit by my side at the meetings, furiously taking notes. Isabel bubbled with enthusiasm once the meetings were over, insisting I was doing well, even when I felt like I'd been beating my head against a rock. At the end of a meeting, she'd always say, "Oh, Karen, it was simply a maaaahvelous meeting." Isabel was my biggest cheerleader. Everyone needs a cheerleader, and Isabel was a pure confidence builder.

At virtually any level of service to others—whether you're volunteering at the local soup kitchen or establishing a charitable organization—you will encounter obstacles along the way. Maybe you can't find the right fit with a partner to create what you want to offer, or perhaps someone doesn't share your vision, a competing plan is implemented, or the organization you wish to volunteer for is so overburdened that they can't even return your call to volunteer. When helping people, know there will be obstacles and opposition, so you may need to tighten up your plan and be prepared to stand up for what you believe in. Remember all the people in need and all the cheerleaders who are counting on you not to give up!

Though initially I'd hoped to find a building we could renovate, I soon realized God didn't want me to find just a building, He wanted me to build community. Having some members on the board as an obstacle to this approach was frustrating, but in the end, they were tremendously beneficial. By challenging my vision, they caused me to ensure my plan was irrefutable and that uniting twelve congregations would serve my purpose of providing shelter to thousands of families in the long run. There's nothing like a bit of resistance to help you perform at your highest level. When I decided to look at my obstacles as opportunities, I felt confident I'd accomplish more than ever.

The resistance from several board members against providing direct service constituted one of the most emotionally exhausting hurdles I had ever encountered. Rather than walk away, I stepped back and traveled to the Bahamas, where I checked into a hotel for a few days to regroup and recalibrate. After soaking in the coastal breeze and taking a leisurely, thought-provoking stroll, I got breakfast in the hotel restaurant and had a wonderful conversation with my server. I told her I wanted to attend church and asked if she knew of any.

Initially, the woman pointed me to a couple of congregations near the hotel, but I was searching for something else. Finally, I paused and told her, "I want to travel to an *old* place in the country," explaining it was because I yearned for a genuine experience. As if she knew precisely what I needed, she smiled softly and nodded before kindly giving me directions to another church.

I finished breakfast, hopped on the motorbike I'd rented, and rode off. But somehow, I managed to get lost and thought I'd never find the church. Suddenly, I heard a burst of music echoing from the second level of an old storefront in a strip mall, and I came to a halt, while my eyes scanned the building. I looked up, thinking it certainly wasn't the stone church the server had told me about. But that didn't stop me. I was inherently drawn to it. After parking my motorbike, I went inside.

Climbing a flight of stairs, I followed the music trail and entered the room from which the music had escaped. A woman introduced herself as Irene and invited me to join them. I was the only Caucasian in the church, but no one seemed to care. They were gathered for one purpose: to praise God. Then, when it was time for prayer, whoever had a concern would go up to the front of the room and state that concern. Several congregation members would lay hands on that individual and pray.

Irene, whom I'd briefly met, gently suggested, "Why don't you go up, Karen?" So, I did.

When asked about my concern, I confessed, "I'm trying to build a shelter for families in need, but I'm experiencing a lot of opposition."

When I glanced around, I could tell by the expressions on people's faces that they also knew there was a need to shelter the homeless, and they seemed pleased with what I wanted to do. And before I knew it, they were praying for me, and some laid hands on me. The sound of their voices was deafening yet peaceful. Cathartic and healing for my soul.

After the service, Irene and her friend Bea escorted me into a smaller room in the back and prayed over me some more. Irene held her hands against the upper part of my chest and began widening my shoulders when I suddenly started speaking in tongues. I never believed in this phenomenon, but I could not deny this garbled speech that seemed to arise from the core of my being. Clearly it was something spiritual. Looking up at the storefront an hour earlier, I'd had no idea I would encounter that type of experience once inside, but God knew.

Before I left, Irene handed me a check for $100. "For your new project," she insisted, then with unwavering conviction, she added, "You just wait and see what God is going to do through you and for you. You are going to help millions!"

CHAPTER 7

When We Open Our Hearts, Lives Are Changed

> May I never get too busy in my own affairs that I fail to respond to the needs of others with kindness and compassion.
>
> —Thomas Jefferson

When the Interfaith Hospitality Network program began on October 26, 1986, at Christ Church in Summit, New Jersey, we converted classrooms into bedrooms, provided home-cooked meals for the families, and had compassionate volunteers on hand who made sure every guest was treated with care and respect.

We knew in advance that we would also need to provide a place for the families to go during the day because we didn't want to be like other shelters and turn them away after breakfast, leaving them to wander the streets. The YMCA in Elizabeth, a few miles away, agreed to provide space in their building, which became our day center. There was room at the

YMCA for up to five families to rest, make phone calls, and receive other social services.

The third challenge we faced was securing transportation so families could travel from the day center to the various host congregations that would house them. After a meeting with the Hyde and Watson Foundation in New Jersey, they gave us a grant to purchase a van. I went to Autoland and shared our story and purpose with them, and they, too, liked what we were doing and gave us a generous discount on a fourteen-passenger van to drive our families around. With a solid business plan, a lot of creativity and compassion, generosity from others, and faith, we pulled together existing community resources to provide shelter, meals, transportation, and other necessities.

As word spread about our services, we soon experienced an influx of families seeking assistance. People often asked me how we arrived at the capacity of fourteen people for our program. I would chuckle, saying, "It's simple. The van only has fourteen seats!"

In Union County, volunteers welcomed our first guests, two single mothers named Cheryl and Margaret and their children, with open arms and hearts. As the women and kids met the volunteers, their initial apprehension seemed to fade. We did everything with kindness and acceptance. Margaret told me, "When I entered the program, it was nothing like a shelter. I had never met such caring people. They treated me like family." Some of our guests have formed long-lasting relationships with our volunteers over the years. Margaret is one such guest. She is still in touch with Anita Nielsen, who helped at the initial conference over thirty years ago that got the ball rolling for the Network.

Our plan was for the host congregation to provide clean

and safe overnight lodging with nutritious meals for up to five families, or fourteen guests, for one week every three months. At the end of the first host week at Christ Church, Pastor Mark said, "The volunteers and our congregation got so much in return. This whole experience was so rewarding to see how we can make a difference in someone's life."

Social service agencies began referring families to us, knowing we had a shelter and other resources to help families in need. Others heard of our first year's success, with 70 percent of our guests finding housing, thanks not only to the case management staff at the agencies that worked with us but also to all the help they received from our volunteers. The spread of the Interfaith Hospitality Network was on its way.

Carl Boast from Prospect Presbyterian in Essex County was the first to collaborate with us and introduce the Network to his congregation, followed by Terry Rehill from St. Patrick's in Morris County. I presented our program to their congregations and addressed their concerns and ideas. Both groups enthusiastically embraced the idea of hosting homeless families in their respective church buildings. Compassion was alive and well!

Some Christian-oriented shelters require their guests to undertake daily Bible study, and everyone has to profess where they stand with the Lord if they want to stay there. By contrast, we were interfaith and believed that all faiths, whether based on the Bible, the Torah, or the Quran, agree on helping the less fortunate. Our purpose was purely to lend a helping hand for folks in need. At the time, there wasn't a mosque involved in the Network, but eventually we grew to have several. Every religious community that joined us saw an opportunity to make a big difference.

I've spoken to many people over the years who have told me they would like to do more for others but don't feel they have any desirable skills or talents to offer. Curious, I will ask them about their interests and hobbies, only to uncover things that those in need would find extraordinarily useful, such as quilt making. One of the congregations in the Network had a quilt ministry and made quilts for the guest families.

Volunteers shared their respective skill sets. Some did nails and others cut hair, which helped guests prepare themselves appearance-wise to return to work if they were out of work. Another volunteer, a photographer, offered to take family portraits. The parents were overcome with joy to receive such a meaningful gift.

When people would tell me they doubted they had any useful skills to contribute, I often gave them examples they hadn't thought of. For instance, when you think about what you have to offer as a volunteer, sure, your piano playing may not land you a spot in an orchestra, but believe me, it could delight an elderly group. You may know how to make a delicious meatloaf people would appreciate eating. Furthermore, teaching someone at a shelter how to make a meal may not only feed them that night but may also give them a new recipe they can use after finding permanent housing.

Consider skills, such as your ability to organize or plan, that can help move someone forward in their life. Do not dismiss them. While you might take such proficiencies for granted, someone else may significantly benefit from them.

When the Interfaith Hospitality Network was running in full force, we had a lot of volunteers because there are incalculable numbers of good people in the world. Many had a chance to live out their faith, show kindness, and make a difference by working with us. Some became advocates for public policies that made a real difference for the population we served.

Some of our volunteers had experienced trauma through loss, illness, or hurt. Because of those feelings, they didn't want others to suffer. Giving of themselves was their way of supporting people who had also experienced hurt, such as through the tragic loss of a home. Volunteers everywhere are dedicated to making a difference in the lives of others. It's as simple as people caring about people.

As I was building the IHN organization in Union, Morris, and other surrounding counties, I was encouraged by the responses we got to what we were creating, and the outpouring of volunteers who were generously giving their time to uplift and change the lives in their community.

Seeing the number of families we were impacting, I wrote a letter to the editor of the *New York Times* explaining how we were making a difference in the lives of people experiencing homelessness. After the op-ed ran and people understood how serious the need was, we received several calls from individuals and organizations wanting to start a similar program in their own local communities. After calling on areas like Philadelphia and presenting the program, I met individually with clergy to go into more detail. I was pleased to discover that many were eager to get involved. With the outpouring of enthusiastic volunteers, generous donors, and sponsors, I saw that compassion knows no boundaries. It was then I knew our work was needed in communities across the country.

By 1988, we converted our organization into a national nonprofit, the National Interfaith Hospitality Network. Giving Millie a ham-and-cheese sandwich produced a ripple effect that presented countless people with the opportunity and experience to help others.

There were a few growing pains, but once the program was underway, it became apparent that something truly extraordinary was happening. It was a movement. People across the United States cared deeply and had an innate desire to contribute and make a difference in the lives of others if given a chance. They just needed to be shown a way to connect. Initially, volunteers started by providing shelter and meals, but as they got to know better the families, who were their guests, they began devising more innovative ways to help. It was truly inspiring to witness the growth of human potential. Most surprising to me was how much the volunteers gained from helping the families.

It took a while for us to understand the magnitude of what was happening. We had accidentally discovered a vast resource of compassion lying dormant in America, waiting to be unleashed. In the almost four ensuing decades, if we counted our volunteers as employees, we would actually represent the thirty-first largest employer in the country, just behind Ford and in front of Disney and Costco.

Many compassionate individuals were eager to provide hospitality in their churches, synagogues, and mosques; cook meals; provide beds; forge friendships; and help people turn their lives around. Parents were thrilled to bring their children along to play with the guests, read to toddlers, or mentor someone in need. As volunteers got to know the guests, they discovered other needs, and many went above and beyond what was required of them. Some helped guests find permanent housing, wrote resumes, donated cars, and secured employment, even offering them job opportunities in their own companies. None of these actions were part of the volunteer manual, but the volunteers felt compelled to do more to uplift their guests.

Our guests could stay overnight for a week in one congregation, starting on a Sunday. The following Sunday, they would pack up and move to the next host congregation. Saying goodbye was never easy for the volunteers, and many would show up at the next location to continue offering support. We were able to share the responsibility by having families stay at different congregations in each community. An added benefit was that the day center could become their permanent address, allowing children to attend school in the same town and ensuring their education remained stable.

In every locality we targeted, we made sure to thoroughly articulate the gravity of the problem, propose plausible solutions, and maintain transparency in all our communications. Upon gaining a clearer understanding of the urgent necessity for our rapidly expanding program, the response was awe-inspiring. An extraordinary number of individuals volunteered, generously donating not only their time and unique skill sets but also, in some instances, their personal funds. It was astounding to observe the extent to which these volunteers were willing to purchase food, clothing, and other necessary supplies, or even amass collections of essential items, all in the hopes of radically transforming the lives of these families grappling with homelessness.

What we had fostered was not a mere collection of individuals but a robust, empathetic community. I have been privileged to witness the restorative and transformative power of compassion in action. The simple acts of giving and caring have an astonishing capacity not only to change lives pragmatically but also to heal deep-seated emotional wounds, bringing about a profound sense of renewed hope and restored dignity to those who once felt abandoned by society.

In order to grow and replicate the success of Union, Essex, and Morris counties in New Jersey on a national scale, we developed an outreach protocol. I had interns call social service agencies to get factual information and conduct assessments in areas to confirm there was a dire need in the target community. Identifying the need allowed us to speak firsthand with accuracy about their specific community when we presented our program to congregations who lived there.

Additionally, we had two or three individuals recruit congregations and people in each community, and then we taught them how to build their local boards and raise money. No one told me how to start an organization and grow it—I did this all on instinct and continued to learn as I dug in. I persevered and relied on God to give me resilience whenever I didn't know where things were heading.

Given that I needed people to introduce the program in new areas across the country and couldn't be everywhere, I created a manual on developing the Interfaith Hospitality Network. Initially, it was merely a document with information void of a detailed process. Then, I turned to the Kellogg Foundation and pitched what we were doing. I told Joel Oroz, the gentleman responsible for philanthropy and volunteerism, that I would be in the area and would love to share the program with them. After speaking with Joel, he said, "It's amazing how you've been able to help so many families, but what I'm most interested in is the number of volunteers you have been able to recruit. That's what I want to fund!" As a result, they gave us a grant of $120,000 to further promote the organization and train new volunteers.

I continued working passionately in many capacities. I was the liaison between the board and the host congregations, did fundraising through public speaking and meeting with foundations and corporations, developed our training manuals, and oversaw the hiring of staff. As new local affiliates were created, I visited them and spoke at their openings. In essence, I had the responsibilities of running a corporation, only on a much smaller scale. Even as we grew, I never forgot that our purpose was to help get families back on their feet, off the streets, and into a warm, safe home. The Network had a 70 percent success rate for helping families find housing. Today's success rate is 82 percent, thanks to the support of staff and volunteers. Other shelters measure success only on bed count per night. Each affiliate of the national network retained local ownership.

As individual affiliates across the country began to understand the needs of their guests and developed additional initiatives to support them, we recognized we had outgrown our original name. We were offering more than just shelter. That's why, in 2003, we changed our name from the National Interfaith Hospitality Network to Family Promise.

I liked the word *promise* because it represented our understanding that families everywhere have potential and promise that can emerge if they receive the right help, and also that our volunteers were making a promise to do whatever they can to help the families achieve sustainable independence.

When the name changed, the organization promised to walk alongside families in their time of need. The name was perfect.

There Are No "Justs"

Volunteers don't always understand the difference they make. I often hear "I just prepare a meal," "I just stay overnight," "I just set up or take down beds," "I just read a story to a toddler," or "I just lend a listening ear."

There are no "justs." Everything that volunteers do helps families get back on their feet. You may not be there when the family turns the key in the door to their new home, but you will have helped all along the way to make that possible.

CHAPTER 8

The Power of Compassion

For it is in the giving that we receive.
—Saint Francis of Assisi

There is always something we can do to extend a helping hand to others, no matter what the specifics of our circumstances and others might be. It feels good to people when we express empathy and compassion. Sometimes, that is enough for them to make changes in their lives.

In the grand scheme of things, our kindness can ignite a spark of hope, a beacon of faith in their otherwise challenging existence. Through these seemingly small gestures, we contribute to the more significant effort of reintegrating people in need into the fabric of society, reinforcing the belief in their ability to reclaim control over their lives and confidently navigate toward a better future.

Over the years, I have met so many people and heard so many stories on the healing impact of kindness, compassion, and caring for others that in the remainder of the book, I have chosen to share some of their stories with you, interwoven with my own anecdotes. It is my hope that you will see how the path of compassion often expands beyond the initial giver to a whole network of individuals. These voices expressing various paths of overcoming hardship with a helping hand from strangers who become friends are reminders of how an act of kindness toward someone in need often creates a grateful heart and the desire to pay it forward. I hope they move you as much as they move me.

We all have the impulse in us to be compassionate. Born into the harsh reality of poverty in Virginia, Shonda Brooks was someone I met who volunteered for Family Promise. Due to her personal experience with homelessness as a child, Shonda knows what it feels like to sleep outside on a freezing-cold night and to wander from shelter to shelter. Sadly, she also knows what it feels like to suffer parental neglect, because her mother was too mentally ill to properly tend to Shonda's needs and her father died when she was quite young. Her childhood memories are painted with stressful images of curling up on park benches to get some sleep on winter nights, where the icy drafts of wind were companions to her fright and uncertainty. Fear clung to her like a second skin as the unpredictability of every tomorrow cast long, daunting shadows on her days. Some nights were a test of endurance, as she learned what it felt like to be fatigued to the bone yet denied the sanctuary of a secure and warm place to rest.

Each move from shelter to shelter etched a scar onto her young heart, leaving her with an enduring reminder of her circumstances. But Shonda was driven to rise above the chaos of her childhood. And the amazing thing is, she has not only survived and thrived, but she has also made it her life's goal to give back to others struggling through similar trials and to teach her children to care for the less fortunate.

SHONDA

My mother was in foster care when I was born. My father died when I was six, and Mom and I bounced from state to state as I struggled to stay connected with her despite her dysfunction. See, my mother had a mental-health disorder that remained undiagnosed for a long time. And even after receiving the diagnosis of bipolar disorder, she wasn't compliant with medication or therapy, which made growing up in her care tough on me. Whenever possible, my mother would arrange for me to stay for a few weeks at the home of a friend, a church pastor, or a relative, but I struggled with the anxiety of being left alone or behind.

Much of my early life revolved around survival, mainly when we lived in the park. When we slept on park benches, we took shifts being a lookout out of fear of being robbed, taken, or injured. When we stayed at the local shelter, Mom and I had to be up and out by 6:00 a.m., and we were not permitted to return until 6:00 p.m. Since I didn't have to be at school until 8:00 a.m., we'd have to wander around town or sit at the bus stop for two hours.

One of the people I stayed with was an older grandmotherly woman from church, Dr. Rose Bland. Dr. Bland took me in and gave me everything a child is supposed to have. An educator, she taught me how to read, helped me with my homework, and even taught me how to tie my shoes. I had a warm bed in which to rest my head at night, but I was terrified to sleep alone, so, many times, I'd crawl into Dr. Bland's bed and sleep beside her.

After staying a couple of months, Dr. Bland asked my mother if she could adopt me. Initially, Mom agreed, but the day before the court appearance, she changed her mind. Dr. Bland took me to see my mother, and when we arrived, Mom made my visit wonderful. Essentially, she enticed me into wanting to live with her. Given she was my mother and had never treated me that way before, I cried and pitched a fit to stay with Mom. Dr. Bland wanted only what was best for me. She said, "I cannot pull a child away from her mother if she wants to stay. All I want to do is help."

Soon after I moved back in with Mom, things went downhill again. Her mental-health crises affected her ability to keep a job and a place to live. With my mom's bipolar disorder, I never knew what to expect from day to day or hour to hour. This took a toll on my own mental health. I spent years struggling with depression and attempted suicide several times. Feeling angry with God, I kept asking, "Why would you put me here to be homeless? I don't understand it. Why would you keep me here?" The last time I asked it, I heard God respond, "It's not your time to go. What are you going to do with this life I've given you?" That question got my attention.

Education gave me a chance to bond with people in a way I couldn't with my mom. Dr. Bland drove home to me how important education was. She said, "You need to have something to bring to the table as a homeless Black girl to make sure people take you seriously. Nobody is going to give you anything free in life, so you have to educate yourself in a way that helps you go out and get things you need and want for yourself." Dr. Bland also helped me get into college. By the time I was ready, she had set aside money for my books and refinanced her house so she could pay my tuition.

Throughout my teens and twenties, I fought to survive and create my own identity. I took the pain from my childhood, turned it around, and used it as an example of what not to do in adulthood. I worked on and off and earned my associate's degree of applied science in business from Bryant & Stratton College. And more importantly to me, I renewed my faith in God.

After years of struggling, I moved to New Jersey, where I met and fell in love with Kelvin, a pastor and a 911 dispatcher and lieutenant for the Plainfield Police Department. After we were married, we started our family, and I continued my studies in psychology, earning a bachelor's degree from Thomas Edison State University. While my kids were little, I taught at a private preschool and led the teen ministry at our church. This connected me with Family Promise.

Our pastor mentioned that our church served as a Family Promise host church, providing homeless families with food and shelter until they could get back on their feet. That appealed to me. I remember preparing and serving dinner for our guests the first time. We sat down with the families and ate while engaging in conversation. Right off the bat, I had moms sharing intimate stories about their lives. After they shared, I asked if I could hang out with their kids in the common area to read them some stories and play with them. I wanted to give the parents a moment to sit at the dinner table and just be adults and relax. They agreed. I took my kids over to the common area, and we played with the visiting children, and it was amazing. It was the most fulfilling thing I'd done in a very long time, outside of getting married and having my children.

For two weeks after that first experience at Family Promise, my soul was unsettled, because I knew I needed to do more. I couldn't sleep over it. I kept telling my husband, "We have to do more than just feed them," and then I connected with the executive director, Geleen Donovan. After Geleen learned all about my history, education, and teaching experience, she explained that she had two lofty dreams for Family Promise of Union County, both of which were right up my alley. The first dream was to provide mental-health counseling services to the parents. I was studying to become a therapist at the time.

The second dream was to start a literacy program. With grant money, Geleen had purchased dozens of children's books, but she had no one to create and run a literacy program. So, I took the books home and produced close to twenty lesson plans for children within three days, one to go along with each book. Geleen was impressed. I then did a ton of research and founded TheNeed2Read, which is a weekly literacy program servicing homeless youth. I also created a detailed plan to attract and train volunteers to launch the program.

Upon reflection, it is evident I was born to work with the families at Family Promise. I was supposed to have the early experiences I did so I could be a consistent, sympathetic presence in these families' lives. Sometimes, we are the most consistent people they see.

After I got a master's degree in professional counseling, I became a licensed clinician and went back for a doctoral degree. Everything awful I had experienced in my life—the uncertainty, the fear, and the anxiety—was eventually eclipsed by the love, direction, and encouragement I received from certain compassionate people. And because I was counseled by loving, compassionate people, I knew I wanted to be that person for someone else.

A few years ago, I took a leap of faith and started my own faith-based counseling practice, River in Eden Counseling, which provides services to diverse individuals. At River in Eden, we are proud to give back to our community through the provision of free or deeply discounted counseling. And not only do we offer free and reduced rates, but we also offer the convenience of virtual sessions.

I vividly recall hoping I could talk to someone outside of my home to help me deal with the issues that arose from having a rough upbringing and a mentally ill parent, and often being met with an outright no for an answer. Sometimes I was brushed off with a quick mention of no one having the time or money to send me to therapy. I want to do the opposite.

I strive to make my counseling practice feel like a family for both my employees and our clients. A family is somewhere you can make mistakes and still be loved, somewhere you are respected, valued, and accepted. Somewhere you feel connected. Because I lacked these things growing up, I value having the opportunity to help others through their struggles. In our practice, we have served more than 400 individuals and 40 families, and the practice is growing. I live with the hope of making a difference in people's lives by giving back everything I didn't have growing up, and then some.

Shonda, Kelvin, and their three children volunteer with Family Promise often, and they address many other needs in their community. It is heartening to see how those who have benefited from acts of compassion, such as Shonda, are often eager to pay it forward and help others in return.

The thing about the power of compassion is that it heals. Whether you're working at a soup kitchen or a shelter, it's the interaction with people that's uplifting. Compassion works miracles. Once you see how what you do impacts others, you may discover there is more you want to do. Ways to show compassion are plentiful. The ripple effect of kindness can be far reaching and can create a chain reaction of kindheartedness that can positively impact countless lives. When we open ourselves to the needs of others and act with empathy and understanding, we create a better world for everyone. Those who have benefited typically don't hesitate to return the blessings.

Volunteering may initially seem daunting in a world characterized by ever-busy lifestyles, work commitments, and family obligations. Yet, as Mary Ryan's story in the following pages illustrates, giving can result in various unexpected and enriching rewards. After an abrupt loss of her eyesight due to diabetes, Mary, instead of wallowing in her circumstances, transcended her adversity to nurture twenty-six newborns and infants over nearly two decades. Her role as a foster parent seemed to render her blindness irrelevant, augmenting the joy and fulfillment from raising her own four sons.

MARY

I woke up at twenty-seven in total darkness one day. This sudden onset of blindness was a result of diabetes, which was diagnosed when I was a child. I had always known I would not let my diagnosis interrupt how I put together my life. I just didn't know what that might have entailed.

The day I woke up in total darkness, I was already a mom of two small children, a nearly three-year-old and a ten-month-old. My husband, John, a lawyer who needed to be in court in Staten Island that morning, turned to me and said, "Mary, I think you're going to be fine here."

I replied, "Okay—we'll see you later, hun."

We were raising our family in my childhood Westfield, New Jersey, home, which I had moved into at age eleven. Nothing had changed in the house, and by the time I was thirty, I knew where everything was by touch.

Over time, our family expanded to include two more children. I have never seen the faces of our third-born son, nor our adopted fourth son. As my four boys grew older, it was important to me to expose them to a world beyond the walls of our home and to teach them to help those in need. I've always felt you've got to help those outside your own family and home. Although there were limited opportunities to volunteer beyond the safety and security of our house, I knew I could find a way to help inside our four walls.

When all our boys were in school, I realized John and I would not have any more infants of our own, but I was fully confident in caring for a fifth child. So, I contacted Catholic Charities to inquire about its need for foster families, specifically offering to foster newborns and infants. I believed being a foster mother would fit my and the baby's needs.

Remember, once you put an infant down, the baby doesn't move. I knew exactly where the cradle and the changing table were. I was fully capable of keeping the baby clean and bottle-fed. Blindness took a back seat on my day-to-day journey, caring for those precious babies.

My days as a foster mom passed just as they did for any other stay-at-home mom. I got my four boys off to school and then spent the remainder of the day caring for the baby and doing household chores, such as folding laundry and putting it away. However, there were a few challenges. When you're blind, you do everything with your hands. Feeding a baby in an infant seat required one hand to hold the baby's hands so they couldn't swat at the food, and a second to find the baby's mouth to put the spoon in. Hungry babies quickly learned how to cooperate!

Schedules, organization, and discipline enabled me to maintain a busy household and provide a loving environment for all of us. I could hear the babies' gurgles and feel their smiles, but I chose not to let my inability to see their faces hinder my ability to care for them. There wasn't time to dwell on that, and I never felt sorry for myself.

We are all disabled, whether emotionally, psychologically, medically, or spiritually. The definition of a disability is anything that makes you susceptible, that brings you to the point of less independence. Blindness certainly fits that bill. But I decided that blindness would not limit my autonomy. Blindness took from me my vision. If I allowed it to take my independence as well, then blindness would no longer be solely a lack of sight. And that's how I live. I never felt blindness was me. I don't feel swamped by it. I don't feel burdened by it. I keep moving on.

During those decades dedicated to fostering, I met many wonderful people and learned how strong I could be. I used that strength a lot. If I could do this, then anybody could do this. I leaned on my extended family, who continually supported me and gave me confidence. Fostering brought great joy to my kids, John, and me.

Fostering not only helped those precious babies thrive, but it also impacted our family and our community. Each time they entrusted a baby to my care, I was thinking about my four boys. I wanted to provide an example of helping others that they could learn from and live by. Three of my sons have expressed interest in fostering. After seeing our extended family participate in church activities, several parishioners in our church also felt the call to become foster parents. It must have occurred to them, "Well, if Mary can do it, so can I."

Through fostering, I've experienced the overwhelming joy of giving a child to a family. Parenting is an awesome responsibility, and I was blessed to take on some of that work. It made me even more conscious that there is work for all of us to do. I may not have created the baby, but I knew what it felt like to give a waiting family a new baby. There's nothing better than that.

Mary graciously took on a role to help someone other than herself and experienced the joy of fulfillment, knowing that her care made a difference in those little babies' lives. Compassion has a way of spreading and inspiring others to act with kindness and generosity. I have always believed that most people are inherently compassionate and want to help those in need, no matter the circumstances. When we create opportunities to assist people, our collective compassion can attract others to join the cause.

CHAPTER 9

The Kindness of Strangers

> The gift of kindness can be felt long after it has been received.
>
> —Linda Poindexter

Long before I started Family Promise, I began volunteering at Greystone State Psychiatric Hospital. At the time, I was a young working mother with two boys. I started working there because it was just down the road from my office at Warner Lambert, and I continued to think of my mother and how she had suffered. I wanted to make a difference in someone's life.

The imposing Greystone State Psychiatric Hospital was established in 1876 and had a haunting stone edifice. As I slowly navigated my way up to the third floor of the spooky, sometimes eerily silent building, the strong scent of urine, bleach, and pain lingered in the air. I got used to this when I visited. Patients were left sitting alone in one big room, some rocking back and forth, others just staring into space. They were together but alone in their pain. Over my sixteen visits,

I met and formed bonds with the patients, many of whom carried tales of family abandonment. Their stories resonated with me and drove home the isolation and loneliness they had been subjected to. Each encounter was a stark reminder of the profound human need for connection, compassion, and care—something these neglected individuals were bereft of in the face of their mental-health struggles.

My time at Greystone was unforgettable. Some patients lived in what were called "cottages." This is where I met Pat, a sweet woman who, most likely, would be at Greystone for the rest of her life. Pat's simple and friendly nature left an indelible impression on me. Since she was in a cottage, I could take her home with me, with permission from the hospital. So, I welcomed Pat back to our house, where I introduced her to Gaga and took her on shopping trips and out to eat. However, I couldn't help but feel there was still so much more I could do for the other patients who were heavily medicated or too out of it to leave with me. So, I sat and drew a sketch of Mary, another patient there. I wanted to leave Mary with something beautiful. Something that could bring her joy. When the sketch was completed and Mary stood over my shoulder gazing at it, she said, "Thank you so much, Karen. I will treasure it."

Despite my numerous visits to volunteer at Greystone, I still felt a void in my soul. The patients I saw in those wards needed help, and I wanted to do more. I tried to humanize their existence and be a light for someone. For a few years, I had been unhappy due to postpartum depression and the breakup of my marriage; it was a challenging time. Through those experiences, I discovered how difficult it can be to pull oneself up, especially when doing it alone.

When Brad was four and Doug was two, during their naps, I made time to paint on a 3-by-4-foot canvas a serene field of colorful flowers with a flowing path leading upward, beneath a pastel-colored skyline. Painting this scene was extraordinarily inspirational when I was battling depression, but looking at it, one would never know I was depressed at the time. It was tranquil and beautiful.

Symbolically, that painting was a reflection of what was to come. What I saw, at some level, is what my spirit saw my future could be. I have it hanging in my home, and it inspires me now as much as it did when I first painted it.

Although painting was a healthy outlet, there's nothing quite as warm and uplifting as the sincerity that the instinctive kindness of a stranger can bring. For example, when I was deeply depressed, a woman from one of the other buildings in my complex stopped me to say hello.

"You always look so sad," she said, noticing something others hadn't. If they *had* noticed, no one had ever said anything.

"Yes," I replied, "I am."

"You know," she began, "I start every morning with prayer and reading the Bible. Why don't you join me? We'll have a cup of coffee together and pray."

I did this for several months. The sincere kindness of this stranger lifted my spirits and reminded me of the power of human connection. I've never forgotten that small act of kindness from a complete stranger. She was already busy, looking after a handful of kids of her own, and still found the time to reach out to someone she could see was hurting.

At another particularly low point in my life, I knocked on the door of a Lutheran church. Desperate and disconnected from church, I was driving down the road and saw a church set back from the street. It was an older redbrick building. I felt led to go and knock on its doors. Even though I wasn't a member of their congregation and the young pastor, with light-brown hair and kind eyes, had never met me before, he greeted me with enormous kindness. I told him I was extremely depressed and needed to talk to someone. Not only did he take the time to listen to me, but he also took the practical step of finding out what interested me. Thinking of my bond with my mother, I told him: swimming. Remarkably, the pastor actually bought me a membership to the YMCA in town. I cried as I swam, but no one could see. I saw the pastor there, too, and we acknowledged one another but didn't speak. He surely knew I was working out the pain.

———

Small acts of kindness can impact and influence how we view others. Time and again, guests of the Family Promise program have commented on how surprised they were by the goodwill of the volunteers, people who didn't even know them but were willing to be welcoming, friendly, and helpful. People struggling with a lack of self-worth or feeling rejected by their family and friends can feel uplifted and valued. Whether giving back to others to reciprocate what has been done for you or simply because you feel it's necessary or right, kindness to a stranger is a powerful gesture for good.

The truth is that all of us need help at some point. The thing to remember is that when we feel alone, there is always someone willing to extend a hand to us, and it may come from the most unexpected person or place. Although accepting help can be humbling, it's all right to let yourself be supported, because someday you can pay it forward to someone else. We need each other. The support we receive from others can bring us hope for a life healthy, whole, and happy again, perhaps in ways that are better than we ever imagined!

Isaac's story is an extreme and remarkable example of this principle of accepting kindness from strangers. His journey began in a tiny, rural village in Ghana, West Africa, where he and his family were immersed in poverty. He was the oldest of three boys. They drank and bathed in contaminated water, and food was always scarce. Life was not easy on a normal day, and sadly, Isaac suffered from an undiagnosed infection in his left arm that left it swollen and with a putrid smell.

ISAAC

My arm was so diseased that I was no longer allowed in the village during the daytime. I was left to die, with my family desperately trying to keep me alive in the middle of nowhere. It took my father two weeks to find someone who could transport me to the hospital in the nearest city. Nothing short of a miracle, a kind stranger agreed to take me, after my father gave him all the money he had, hence commencing the series of miracles that saved my life through the kindness of strangers.

When I arrived at the hospital, my father managed to convince the staff to treat me, promising that he would return to pay for the treatment. My dad did return, as promised, but when he did, he shared the devastating news that my youngest brother had died of malnutrition. That visit was the last time I set eyes on my father and other brother. I never saw them or my mother again. I was only six years old.

I spent several years at that hospital with doctors doing multiple surgeries and treatments on my infected arm. My fortunes took a turn when a nurse supervisor, Martha Mary, noticed me and became my guardian angel. She provided me with food and new clothes and ensured my well-being. It was the first time in my life I remember experiencing genuine kindness.

When the time came for me to be discharged, the plan was to send me to a nursing home. Martha Mary, who had become a motherly figure to me, intervened, demonstrating unparalleled love and compassion, and introduced me to a missionary named Rebecca from the organization Healing the Children. After she met me, Rebecca arranged to send me to the United States. This was the first of many such trips to receive medical treatment. On the first trip, I received exceptional care at St. Jude's Hospital. There, I met Carol Lucas, an administrator at the hospital, who would spend her day off teaching me English.

Before I went back to Ghana, Healing the Children arranged for a host mother, Pauline, to care for me. Pauline introduced me to the American way of life, and I cherished every minute of the adventure. Her friend, Mary Ryan, who I called Auntie Mary, would become another important figure in my life.

Rebecca obtained a new visa for me. On my second trip to the States, I was admitted to Shriners Children's Hospital in Chicago. It was there, at age fourteen, that I had to make a momentous decision to amputate my arm or face death. Rebecca's comforting presence got me through feeling alone and scared. While I was recovering and undergoing physical therapy at Shriners, I was visited by a group of strangers who told me, "Mary Ryan sent us." She had heard I was back in the States and sent her family to check on me. I remembered Auntie Mary right away and was thrilled to receive an invitation to stay with her and her family for the summer in Westfield, New Jersey.

Auntie Mary had been in contact with a missionary couple who, having previously worked with Rebecca in Ghana, now resided just an hour away in Pennsylvania. The couple, Chuck and Dawn, visited me on several occasions before extending an invitation to live with them. When I was sixteen, they adopted me.

I was so excited to have a loving family and the opportunity to be properly educated. My parents would tirelessly sit by my side until late at night, guiding me through my schoolwork, supporting me when I wanted to give up, and helping me cope when I had feelings of not belonging. They exemplified pure love and unwavering support until the day they passed away.

I look back on my life now, acknowledging, cherishing, and showing gratitude to all the strangers who showed me kindness. None were deterred by the challenges I faced, and they became a conduit for miracles for me. Without their divine interventions and those of God, I would not be where I am today. I am currently working as a custodian. I am also volunteering at a hospital's outreach program, and I have been working toward my bachelor's degree in social services, because I hope to share the kindness that was given to me and be the miracle in the life of someone else.

People may come and go, but it is the impact they make when they are present that matters. You may never know if what you have done has made a significant change in someone's life. It shouldn't matter. Offer a helping hand when you see the need. Value everyone you meet.

CHAPTER 10

Hope Found

> Sometimes good things fall apart so better things can fall together.
> —Marilyn Monroe

When I arranged to meet Hope, a former Family Promise guest, and her bubbly three-year-old daughter, Olivia, on a sunny day, we sat in a park and spoke about their journey for an hour and a half. Hope pulled a few toys from her purse. If Olivia became bored with the other toys, I brought cars and trucks for her to play with—along with a cake.

I sensed Hope's gratitude, and she captured my full attention as she told me her story, allowing me to see a glimpse of something long since behind her. Hope's story was nothing short of heart-wrenching and miraculous, interwoven with the reminder to never underestimate the power of kindness. As Maya Angelou wrote, "I've learned that people will forget what you said, people will forget what you did, but people will never forget how you made them feel."

HOPE

Homelessness can happen to anyone, and in 2010, although I didn't have any of the problems people often stereotypically associate with homelessness, it found me. I wasn't an addict or an alcoholic, and I wasn't struggling with mental health; I was a single mother working long hours as a waitress to support my one-year-old daughter, Olivia. After rebounding from a divorce and recovering from a previous mentally and physically abusive relationship, I was without a family support system or a strong network. I come from a blue-collar family in Hunterdon County, New Jersey, one of the wealthiest counties in the country. When I had my daughter, my parents believed I had chosen my path and left me to figure life out. I was okay with that, because I knew that was how I would grow, but I had no idea just how much.

Things were good with Olivia and me until the morning I woke up and instantly knew something was wrong. My eyes were blurry and didn't get any better when I rubbed them. I kept rubbing them as though I was cleaning the cornea, but still, no improvement. I could see light and could tell that I was in a room, but I couldn't see anything else. By the time I'd fumbled around, dressing Olivia for daycare and getting ready for work, I still couldn't see that well. It seemed I'd lost my peripheral vision first, then my total vision. Assuming the problem was temporary and knowing I couldn't miss work, I drove, since it wasn't far away. My eyesight was comparable to having frost on a windshield obstructing the view.

When I got to work, my coworkers told me my eyes were bleeding, and one of my girlfriends drove me to a doctor near the restaurant. After a thorough examination, the doctor suspected I had contracted a virus from a strain of something Olivia had brought home from daycare. I had Olivia checked out, too, and was grateful when the doctor said she was unaffected.

Although doctors and specialists insisted the blindness was temporary, they said it could take as long as six months to regain my vision. I was terrified. Then, to make matters worse, I had an allergic reaction to the prescription they gave me—the eye drops didn't help, and my vision hadn't improved after two weeks. Just to manage, I called a lady who lived a street over to help me change Olivia's diaper to ensure I was cleaning her thoroughly and dressing her well. There were days when the most I could see were shadows and shapes a mere four or five inches in front of my face. My daughter was so young that I realized I couldn't care for her the way I needed. I felt hopeless.

Discouraged, I didn't believe I'd be able to see again. I lost my driver's license and was forced to quit my job. Suddenly, the injury to my eyes and health issues beyond my control drastically changed my life, putting me at risk of losing everything.

The only option I had was to inquire about receiving disability benefits to keep from losing my apartment and to be able to take care of Olivia. I couldn't get a straight answer from anyone. Finally, I was connected with Debbie, a social worker from Norwescap, a multiservice agency, who was genuinely concerned and did everything she could to help us find a solution. Debbie made weekly visits to check on us. Unfortunately, although Debbie was doing everything in her power to help us and to buy us time, she couldn't prevent our eviction five months later. Without the means to pay people to help move our personal belongings, I could only salvage what

I could move to a small storage unit: our beds and a few boxes. All else I had to leave behind. I was afraid—I didn't want to be homeless. That was the lowest point in my life.

The day I was evicted from my apartment and had nowhere to go, Debbie came by and told me, "I found someone to help you." She was referring to the Family Promise affiliate in Flemington, New Jersey. After explaining who they were and that we would be well cared for and have shelter, food, and clothing, Debbie generously offered to take us there to introduce us to the staff.

I asked, "Can I think about it?"

Puzzled, Debbie stared at me for a moment with her hands resting on her hips. "Hope, what is there to think about? Do you want to sleep in your car, or do you want to come to Family Promise?"

Debbie's words landed, and I replied, respectfully, "Good point."

I knew those were my only options.

At just twenty-three years old, I was humbled, and deep down, I felt this was now my life. Not knowing what to expect was traumatizing. I had nothing. I had never thought I wouldn't be able to take care of my child. I didn't know how to support her, but losing Olivia wasn't an option.

Seemingly sensing my fear, Debbie took my hand, looked me in the eyes, and said she believed in Family Promise. But at that moment, other than living out of my car, which wouldn't be safe, we had nowhere else to go. The kindness of a stranger helped me to trust an organization I didn't know anything about. I had gotten to know Debbie over the previous months, and she was like a mom to me. She took us there on her own time and ensured we were settled so our healing could begin.

The adjustment on our first night was difficult and heart-wrenching, but although I was experiencing homelessness, I wasn't made to feel that way. We met the kindest people in the days and weeks ahead, including Family Promise executive director Geleen Donovan, case manager Donna Michelsen, and volunteers Lou and April Ambrio and Carol Coriel. They weren't strangers. They were incredible human beings who truly cared about people. They had their own lives and families, yet they believed in me more than I believed in myself. It wasn't just me; I could tell they never stopped believing in anyone who walked through their doors. Their compassion wasn't out of selection, but of humanity. Everyone was given the benefit of the doubt regardless of the path that brought them there.

For the first time, I wasn't left to figure things out on my own. They provided counseling, support, and life skills like budgeting and organization. Perhaps the most crucial: they helped me regain my self-worth. They listened to, loved, and supported us in the kindest and most complete ways. Families brought Olivia diapers and clothing. A woman charitably paid my phone bill so I could look for jobs. I became family to the staff and some of the other volunteers. During that time, amid all the love, compassion, and support, I slowly regained my eyesight.

Determined to help me return to my independent life, Geleen emailed the coordinators in the Family Promise congregations, stating I had an interview with Verizon Wireless. She asked if anyone was willing to donate professional clothing for the interview. Carol called Geleen and said, "I don't have any clothes, but I'd like to take her shopping." Then Carol called me, asking, "Where do you want to meet?"

I said, "How about Kohl's?"

"How about Macy's?"

"Oh good Lord!"

Carol bought me about ten outfits with her own money. And April's husband, Lou, who worked at Verizon, put in a good word for me, and I got the job!

I never understood before how powerful compassion and action are. As a society, we tend to be dismissive of the plight of others until we find ourselves in a similar situation that warrants the compassion of caring human beings who want to see people succeed, with no other agenda. These kind strangers gave me a sense of security and family, which let me know we would be okay and that I could support my daughter without worrying. The generosity of human beings, beginning with Debbie, allowed me to pull my life and self-worth back together after carrying the overwhelming feeling of defeat, the belief that I wasn't a good mom.

Moving forward, Olivia and I continued living at the host congregations; Olivia was in daycare, and I began training and working at Verizon. Again, I had angels looking out for me. April and Lou opened their home to us, but given all the support I had, I was determined to get my own place and show everyone involved in getting me back on my feet that I was a worthwhile investment. I felt like a seedling pushing through the soil, determined to grow and thrive despite the odds. With the right resources, care, and attention, I resolved to make something of myself. I saved everything I could and bought an inexpensive car that didn't have heat or air-conditioning, but I was proud of it because it was a huge accomplishment.

Six months later, I could afford an apartment. Carol again took me shopping and bought us several things I could not have gotten all at once but that we needed—a shower curtain, pots and pans, dishes, and anything she thought we could use.

Seeing the investment so many people made in me, going above and beyond, I worked my butt off and became the manager of a Verizon store. April and Lou became Olivia's godparents and continued to visit us regularly.

When Carol heard I was going to start looking for a better car with heating and AC, she insisted on adding to my budget so I could buy something more reliable. When I found a little Hyundai, I showed it to Carol and her husband, and they helped me buy it. Then, as if that weren't enough, they helped me buy a toaster oven for my new place. The entire experience taught me what compassion for others looked like, what kindness and gratitude are, and what I could do in return. I told them I wanted to do the same—be a light for someone without judging them. I wanted to be a resource and help prevent families and people in general from being homeless.

In keeping with my word, I've spoken at regional and national Family Promise fundraising events and served on its guest advisory board. I've discovered that we really don't know where homeless people are coming from or what they're experiencing or have been through. But being nice and instilling hope in others doesn't take any effort. It's free. And I realized that if I could make one person feel better, I wanted to do that!

My life is better than I ever expected. I met a wonderful man named Bo, who adopted Olivia. We had a child together, and Olivia now has a little brother, James. I get so emotional when I think about my life now. I live in a beautiful home with a beautiful family and am incredibly happy. Losing my eyesight was the journey I was meant to take, because it led me to self-discovery, confidence, and determination. The compassion and care I received was much bigger than I could have ever imagined.

I don't know who selects the staff at Family Promise, but those people don't work for money. They do it because they care about the well-being of their guests. Because of this organization, we have lifelong friends who genuinely care about us. I wouldn't have a healthy relationship, be a good mother, and have another happy baby if it weren't for their volunteers.

When I see how happy and well adjusted Olivia is, playing softball, performing in theater, and making friends, it brings me to tears. Olivia was nine when she heard me speak at a meeting for Family Promise and share our story. Until then, I hadn't told Olivia about our experience of homelessness out of fear she would be embarrassed. But that day, my daughter ran onstage, hugged me, and cried as she told me how much she loved me. Family Promise gave me the tools, and they helped me when I was at my lowest. They encouraged me to support myself, live independently, and take the steps necessary to improve my life. This helped me become a better mom and person because they believed in me, and they do that for so many people.

As a volunteer now at Family Promise, I share my experience through the program with those who offer their time to help the families experiencing homelessness. For example, I've taken a program called Healing From Homelessness that educates staff and volunteers about the traumas experienced when losing your home. It evokes the same feelings of loss as anything else—such as your job or a loved one. A loss is a loss.

The emotions our clients are going through are traumatic, and everyone needs to be aware of how that impacts behaviors and where people are in their lives.

After hearing Hope's story, I couldn't help but observe how well adjusted and happy Olivia was—her smiles and laughter spoke volumes. I saw the love and reassurance her mother gave her and realized that despite their path of having experienced homelessness, her daughter seemed unfazed and incredibly loved.

When people's lives are suddenly flipped upside down, whether due to illness, a disaster, loss, or homelessness, it can significantly impact them. The burden seems a bit lighter with the support of kind, caring people to guide you through. Hope's story is a wonderful illustration of how the gifts of kindness don't cost anything but can bring joy to the hearts of the giver and receiver—and the beautiful thing is the hope we are creating.

We must never forget that the complexities surrounding homelessness cannot be simplified into a single narrative. There are many precipitating reasons for a person to become homeless, such as divorce, loss of a job, illness, or substance abuse, but the root cause in every case is the critical shortage of affordable housing, as the gap between income and the cost of housing continues to grow. In the early 1980s, there were drastic cutbacks to the Housing and Urban Development

(HUD) budget, resulting in decreased availability of housing. Since then, rents have continued to rise, and lower-income people in particular have experienced slow or stagnant wage growth. Currently, for every four people eligible for low-income housing, only one home is available. It is a challenge that requires collaboration and innovation from all sectors of society to address effectively.

The facts are that:

- In the United States, 1 in 30 children experience homelessness annually.[1]
- Approximately 30 percent of the nation's homeless population are families with children. HUD's data is based on a Point-in-Time (PIT) count. That count is restricted to people in shelters, in transitional housing, or on the streets. But most families and youth who are homeless do not stay in shelters, in transitional housing, or on the streets; they stay in motels or temporarily with other people due to lack of alternatives.[2] [3]
- 1.2 million homeless students, preK-12, were recorded from the 2021-2022 school year by the Department of Education.[4]
- The federal minimum wage is $7.25 per hour. It hasn't changed since 2009.[5]
- In no state, metropolitan area, or county in the U.S. can a worker earning the federal or prevailing state or local minimum wage afford a modest two-bedroom rental home at fair market rent.[6]
- Most renting families below the poverty line

now spend at least 50 percent of their income on housing. (The recommended amount to spend on housing is 30 percent of income or less.)[7]
- In 2023, the poverty line for a family of 4 was $30,000 a year.[8]
- Only 1 in 4 of those considered eligible for federal housing assistance receive help, due to lack of funding.[9]
- Nearly 30 million Americans remain completely uninsured a decade after the passage of the Affordable Care Act.[10]

CHAPTER 11

A More Expansive Heart

The best way to find yourself is to lose yourself
in the service of others.

—Mahatma Gandhi

Compassion is an incredibly powerful agent for healing and transformation. If someone has ever been kind to you when you were down, then you know how intensely appreciated support can be. Just the simple act of having someone care for us or be present can touch us and warm our hearts. Because it restores our spirit, kindness and compassion can lift us up and inspire us to change our lives—even leading us to pay it forward and show compassion for someone else.

But as it turns out, compassion is as good for the giver as the receiver. The mental and emotional benefits of compassion go both ways. It doesn't cost a thing to allow our hearts to be moved by another person's predicament. Still, some people are surprised when they discover the depths of their feeling for others and the immensity of the empathy they have when they begin volunteering. They are astonished to see how much their simple generosity affects others.

At Family Promise, we're incredibly grateful for the dedication and generosity of our volunteers. Each and every one of them brings a unique set of skills and qualities that make a real difference in the lives of our guests. Compassion is the quality at the root of all of these.

Pace is a great example of a compassionate person. Despite holding a demanding position as a senior executive at Sandia National Laboratories, he still found the time to volunteer with us and discovered a newfound sense of purpose and fulfillment in the process. His story is a testament to the transformative power of giving back and cultivating a more expansive heart. It's stories like these that shine a light on the remarkable character and empathy of our volunteers. We couldn't do what we do without them, and we're honored to have them by our side.

PACE

In 1993, I was transferred to lead another organization within the laboratory. My associates were throwing me a going-away party. Several people, mainly scientists, stood up to give testimonials; however, I remember only one.

When the scientists had finished talking, a secretary, Alice, whom I did not know well, shyly raised her hand to speak. Alice shared the story of a chance encounter with me several years earlier when I had come to her aid one wintry night when she got a flat tire that left her stranded.

Alice told everyone about that evening. There was a sudden cold snap, and it started sleeting. Before she reached the main road, she pulled over with a flat tire, but a stream of cars continued to pass by, causing her to panic. Alice noticed someone pull up behind her, get out of their car, and knock on her window. It was me. Ignoring the conditions, I went ahead and changed her tire. Alice recalled that I wasn't dressed for the weather but didn't seem to mind. She said, at that point, I stopped being "just a suit" and instead became a human being to her.

I was touched by her thoughtful words, the effect of which extended beyond that party. In the following days, I reflected on how my simple, automatic response to her situation had made such a lasting impact on her. It wasn't significant to me because I'd done this before and had forgotten about the encounter with Alice. However, it was of importance to her. I concluded I could do more to make a difference in people's lives. I didn't want to be known as a "suit." That began a more thorough search for meaningful ways to assist people. Unknowingly, Alice opened my heart to become more expansive.

I got involved with Family Promise when my church, First United Methodist, helped start the Albuquerque affiliate. Due to my hectic schedule, family, work, and church seemed to be the only things I had time for. However, the program appealed to me emotionally, and overnight hosting was something I could fit into my busy life because I still had to sleep. So, in that position, I slept overnight at the church. Then, before I headed to work, I would prepare and serve breakfast.

Every quarter at my church, they select a different coordinator to oversee the program. Very quickly, I recognized the program was suffering from a lack of continuity, so I volunteered to coordinate. In addition, I wanted to contribute some management skills, and I became the program coordinator, a role I was in for more than eleven years.

I have retired from my job at the laboratory and now conduct research on physics that might lead to new energy sources, so I'm working fewer hours. Consequently, that allowed me to devote more hours to Family Promise. I led our congregation's hosting of homeless families by recruiting and coordinating the work of approximately fifty volunteers who provided families with essential respect and loving-kindness as well as food, lodging, and transportation.

When I began helping on weekends, I got to know our guests personally. They would open up to me and, without my asking, tell me their stories. Like Alice did with me, I got to know them as "real people."

On the weekends, I prepared breakfast for our guests and planned recreational activities for families. Our activities ranged from yoga sessions and mountain hikes to bowling, and my wife, Nancy, assisted me with the program. "Hospitality" isn't just a word to use with Family Promise. We invited our guest families to our home. We had a zip line in our backyard that we encouraged them to try. Although it was only about fifteen feet high, it was tall enough to provide our guests with the experience of tackling their fears and persevering. On weekends, we began holding mock job interviews, and these have since been incorporated into the day program that our guests attend. As an experimental physicist, I can fix almost anything, so I helped our guests with car repairs and occasionally organized dinners for volunteers to facilitate training and building rapport. After every hosting, I emailed an after-hosting report to volunteers, sharing significant milestones our guests had reached so they could see how they had touched their lives.

I keep in touch with many of the families we've hosted. I remember one of the first families who graduated from our program. About a month after that hosting, I saw the family in a local restaurant. Their five-year-old son ran up to me and gave me a big hug, which surprised me because I didn't think they would remember me. I deemed it another "Alice experience"—*when we care and act, we make lasting changes in people's lives.*

I have derived meaning and humanity from my experience with Family Promise. Outside of my family, my value system before volunteering extended to what I could do in my professional career. However, I've discovered that guests have incredible stories, and Family Promise has connected me with people who show great courage in facing adversity. I am constantly inspired by the courage our guests bring to their situations. Helping them has been a way to help my humanity grow—a way to show respect for people who have temporarily lost some of their own self-respect.

Since volunteering, I have been more physically, mentally, emotionally, and spiritually alive because our guests gave me something—inspiration. They have inspired me in a way that has helped me open my heart and connect with someone other than my family and coworkers. Because of this, I have a strong desire to help them thrive, which is one way I grow my spirituality. It lets me live with a caring and expansive heart.

Despite no longer being a coordinator, Pace and his wife, Nancy, have remained active advocates for individuals within their community. They have continued to selflessly volunteer their time by preparing Monday-night meals for those in need. However, Pace's compassion does not end there. He has become a reliable resource for guests who require assistance with various issues, from car troubles to other unforeseen challenges. Moreover, Pace has made it his mission to locate safe and stable housing options for those with HIV. He also regularly checks in on one couple, providing them with essential support. The wife has been blind since birth. The husband suffers from brain damage after an accident. Pace continues making a difference in people's lives through his commitment to volunteering his time to help those in need.

———

Having a more expansive heart allowed me to express my heart's longing to make a difference. I started small with Millie. When I got her a sandwich, I sensed she was hurting. Instinctively, I wanted to make a difference, even if it was fleeting. But when Millie took my hand, a beautiful moment transpired between us, encouraging me to go further on my journey. That led me to host the conference on homelessness. I knew what suffering was, and when I saw others in need, I wanted to help.

One day, I was walking in the park near my home and saw this bearded man sleeping on a bench with a bag beside him. Thinking he was homeless, I went to my car and got $20 to give him. Not being a hundred percent certain he was homeless and not wanting to insult him, I decided against giving it to him. A few weeks later, I was outside Dunkin' Donuts, and after seeing the same man again, I asked if he wanted a cup of coffee. He said, "Sure," so I got him a coffee and one for myself and asked if I could sit with him for a minute.

His name was Ed. After talking with him, I discovered he had been on the streets for a few years. Ed didn't want to go to shelters because he thought they were dangerous, opting instead to sleep in the train station or behind a store. When his mother died, he'd inherited $17,000, but he quickly spent it all. I asked if he had a phone, and he didn't, so I gave Ed a ride into town and bought him one, adding it to my account. I thought it could be a lifeline for him, enabling him to keep in touch with the few relatives and friends he had. I told him if he wanted, I could call someone from Union County Social Services, and they could help him. But Ed declined. I thought he had adapted to his situation and didn't want anything more.

I check on Ed from time to time, meeting him at the library or going out to lunch. On one particular occasion, I took Ed out for his birthday. While eating, we talked about sports and the latest book he'd read. When we were finished, the entire waitstaff surrounded our table, delivering a chocolate cake with a candle. They proceeded to joyously sing, "Happy Birthday to Ed," with nearby tables joining in. Ed was so surprised, he exclaimed, "For me?" He then blew out the candle, making a wish.

Ed is a very positive person, despite his situation. When I see him, now and then, I give him $20 or a pair of socks. He often visits the library, where he spends most of his day reading self-help books like *The Power of Positive Thinking*, *The Secret*, and others. Although this has become Ed's way of life, I continue trying to help. Recently, he's been connected with a social worker and now receives food stamps and General Assistance.

I began this chapter talking about how compassion benefits the giver as well as the receiver. I know encounters like the ones I have with Ed nourish me deeply. Even after all these years of advocacy and caring for people who are homeless, I never grow fatigued with reaching out to someone in need. It fills my soul and brings a sense of joy, just being a friend to Ed and helping him get the assistance he needs.

CHAPTER 12

Pain Can Have a Silver Lining

> Out of suffering have emerged the strongest souls; the most massive characters are seared with scars.
>
> —Kahlil Gibran

Throughout our lives, most of us will experience some form of loss or tragedy, or know someone close who has. Though it can be hard to see through the lens of trauma, pain can come with a silver lining. It has the power to create empathy and understanding between people who are going through similar struggles. Pain can sensitize the heart, make us stronger and more resilient, and equip us with the life experience necessary to help others navigate their own traumas.

Life can change in an instant without any warning or time to prepare. It happened to me. And while my experience was not with homelessness, the pain and trauma of losing my mother profoundly altered my life. This tragedy shook me to my core, and I know firsthand that life outside our control can affect us in ways we never anticipate. We often try to work through these adversities in silence, striving to be resilient, but sometimes we are at a loss for a solution. Temporary or permanent, these situations can have mental, emotional, and physical impacts on our lives, and the kindness of others can make a significant difference in our recovery.

Experiencing homelessness can have a profound impact on an individual's confidence and self-worth, leaving them feeling isolated and different from others. However, what can make all the difference is having someone to listen to, encourage, and guide them through challenging times. Volunteers who take the time to connect with guests and offer authentic support are the ones who create meaningful change. Even the smallest compassionate gestures—like sharing a meal or playing with children—can provide a sense of normalcy and belonging to those experiencing homelessness. It's crucial we continue to work together to improve the transition process and ensure no one feels left behind.

In some cases, the line between the "unhoused" and the "housed" is very thin. A young woman wanted to volunteer at her church, so she took her six-year-old daughter with her and explained, "We're going to volunteer and help the homeless." When they arrived, the mother took her daughter to play with the kids. They played tag and with a ball beautifully for a few hours with laughter and giggles. When it was time to leave, her daughter asked sweetly, "When are we going to see the homeless?"

At Family Promise, constant, authentic interactions between guests and caring volunteers have proved to be the healing part of the recipe. That is the secret sauce! If we can work together and continue to find ways to improve someone's transition out of unfavorable conditions, we should. We cannot minimize what others endure.

Pain can have a silver lining. It teaches us and opens our hearts to one another. Joe Ader, the executive director of Family Promise in Spokane, Washington, is an inspiring example of how pain and hardship can be transformed into purpose and compassion. Growing up in a traumatic environment that threatened to derail his life, Joe found solace in a few loving and influential people who helped him navigate a different path.

JOE

In life, we all face dark and disappointing times that can make us question if we will ever find purpose or meaning in our experiences. I had a very violent childhood. My brother physically and sexually abused me, causing insurmountable suffering, which included broken bones and multiple hospital visits. Like most kids who experience abuse, I never talked about it. I simply compartmentalized the pain and let the anger brew just beneath the surface. Adding to my insecurity and shame was that I struggled to read due to dyslexia, forcing me to repeat first grade. That second year of first grade, my teacher, Ms. McElroy, a pastor's wife, recognized my potential. Every day, she kept me in the classroom during lunch and recess, teaching me to read and write. I don't know where I'd be without her. Without a doubt, Ms. McElroy's kindness helped me become successful in many other areas of my life and also gave me an example of what it means to sacrifice in service to others.

My parents, the first generation out of poverty, were hard working. My father was the youngest of seven from an Irish family that had moved from the South Side of Chicago to California. My mother's parents were sharecroppers who survived the Dust Bowl. "Hard working" is an understatement. My father always had multiple jobs, as did my mother. So, this meant we were latchkey kids and also that they weren't around to be fully aware of the abuse I endured. One of my mother's jobs was as a receptionist at a psychiatric hospital. That fit her well because she always had a passion for helping people. At forty-five, my mother started night school to become a social worker. After receiving her undergraduate and master's degrees, she went on to work as a social worker in psychiatric hospitals for the next twenty-three years.

At the same time my mother was taking classes, I was learning how to be a peer counselor. This gave me valuable exposure and insight into people with various backgrounds and perspectives. I began to realize that our own painful experiences and unfavorable circumstances can be used to help others overcome their adversity, heal, find faith, and initiate a powerful and contagious cycle of compassion. Why would we leave anyone in pain?

I think when we've endured some form of insurmountable pain that seems nearly impossible to overcome and have had someone unselfishly help us work through it, it presents us with a higher calling. Often, we want to serve others to return the gift of healing.

In middle school, while I was learning to be a peer

counselor, a pretty girl invited me to church. I went, and let's just say my motivation was not to chase God but that girl. However, God had other plans. It was there that I was saved and accepted Christ. My heart was transformed and a week later I went with that same church group to inner-city Los Angeles, where we met kids whose mothers were prostitutes. That experience ignited a desire in me to learn about poverty so I could better serve others. The desire to learn and help continued into adulthood and eventually propelled me to leave the corporate world to pursue serving those in need full-time.

In 2006, my wife and I moved to Flower Mound, Texas, where we were invited to Bridge Church in Denton, Texas. One thing led to another, and the pastor, Matt Chandler, asked me to accept a job as a missions' pastor. As a requirement for all pastors on staff, I participated in a twelve-step recovery program. Since I didn't drink or abuse substances, I felt I didn't need to be there. However, yet again, God had other plans. In a meeting with my sponsor, he asked, "Well, is there anything else?"

Painful recollections of my abusive childhood played like a movie in my mind, causing me to tell him there was something else. For the first time, I shared with someone about the abuse I had been through. Then I said, "But I am fine now. I have forgiven my brother."

He looked at me for what seemed like a very long time and then said, "Have you told him that?" I had not. In fact, we had never talked about the abuse and the pain. I realized there was a fear there, and that in order to truly overcome the past and not just compartmentalize it, I needed to speak with him about it.

To fully heal from the dark cloud of my past, I knew I

needed to tell my brother I'd forgiven him fully and finally. I flew to California for a funeral my brother was also attending. I invited him to take a walk on the beach so I could tell him the truth. We walked on the cliffs with some outcroppings and found a place to settle, but my brother spoke before I could say anything.

"Bro," he began, "I've been doing a step-studies thing, and one of the steps is to make amends with those you've wronged. I want you to know I'm sorry." He said it with sincere remorse. Having gone through the step program to become a pastor, I understood what he needed to do and why. We talked about it for twenty minutes or so, and I shared the pain I went through and that I forgave him. After all the pain, abuse, and anger I'd harbored over the years, I received a heartfelt apology that allowed me to release these emotions and find relief. It was a deeply cathartic experience.

It's natural to question if our experiences enduring dark and discouraging periods in life could ever be used for good. However, the divine experience as a pastor in Texas allowed me to heal from my trauma, and I wanted to help others do the same. So, after a decade in Texas, my wife and I moved to Washington state to help some friends with their church. A month later, I began working with homeless families for Family Promise. Most of the parents had traumatic childhoods, and I was able to share my story, how I overcame the pain and how pain can be used to help others. At one point, one of the toughest fathers came to me privately and said, "How did you forgive? I don't think I could forgive my dad for what he did to me." That opened a dialogue that helped him walk through his pain and insecurity.

My ability to work through the trauma that many try to

repress led me to an important calling. It has allowed me to connect with others, train others to do the same, and create the most successful program for preventing and ending homelessness in eastern Washington. My story is evidence that the pain you've experienced is not a life sentence. Instead, it can be transformed into a calling that can bring purpose, empower you to make a difference, and help others walk a little easier.

———

It's understandable to wonder if our experiences during life's most challenging and disheartening times could ever serve a higher purpose. Joe's journey is a potent reminder that suffering doesn't have to dictate our life's trajectory. Instead, it can equip us to effect change and inspire others to believe in the possibility of recovery. Because they are aware of what it's like to endure hardship, many individuals who have encountered pain or loss find the motivation to assist others to avoid similar pain. We can all glean wisdom from Joe's path and use our past trials to infuse the world with greater compassion and empathy.

CHAPTER 13

Unexpected Healing

> It is one of the beautiful compensations of life that no man can sincerely help another without helping himself.
>
> —Ralph Waldo Emerson

Individuals and organizations dedicated to service are like lighthouses amid tempestuous storms, radiating beacons of hope and facilitating unforeseen healing for those ensnared in the grasp of loneliness and despair. They provide the fortitude to weather the storm and instill the faith that a safe refuge awaits. In our mission, we aspire to serve as a beacon, offering an abundance of hope and love vital to navigating life's challenges. Strikingly, through this process of providing comfort, we often encounter our own unique form of healing. The impact we make extends far beyond our comprehension, reinforcing the truth that our purpose is profoundly more significant than we can ever fully grasp.

Several years ago, I spoke at the Tenth Anniversary Celebration for Family Promise of Knoxville. When I finished speaking, a woman named Thea, with tears filling her eyes, approached me to thank me for starting the program. She told me we saved her life. Although it's not unusual to hear this from families, until then, I had never heard a volunteer say it. Thea shared how Family Promise came along at just the right time.

THEA

I was married to my husband, Dick, just shy of thirty-three years. For the last five years of his life, he was terminally ill with pulmonary fibrosis, and we placed him into hospice care. He couldn't get out of the house much and needed breathing tubes, and I didn't go out except for necessities. So, it was just the two of us, and everything we experienced became our new normal.

Despite not having a church affiliation at the time, my husband and I took solace in watching Sunday services on TV. As we faced our challenges, we leaned on each other for support and grew spiritually closer as a couple. Though our journey was not an easy one, we made the conscious decision to make the most of every moment we had together. My husband's unwavering positivity and grace in the face of adversity was truly inspiring and left an indelible mark on my heart.

The experience of caring for my husband in his final days was nothing short of heart-wrenching. As my husband's time drew near, the hospice nurse gently prepared us for what would come. My daughter called the rector of her church, St. Andrew's Episcopal Church. Within fifteen minutes, he came to the house, read psalms, and said prayers as my husband passed away. It seemed to happen suddenly.

Even though I am not a member, the church arranged a memorial service for Dick. The church was full of people I didn't know at the service, but they knew my daughter. Given how everything seamlessly unfolded, I felt I needed to be a part of that church. My life had been spent primarily with Dick, and the time I spent at church caused me to shift from having few friends to many. While I was going through a difficult time with the sudden loss of my husband, everyone was supportive and friendly. The church became where I went for peace, and while they had several outreach programs, the opportunity to work with Family Promise grabbed me immediately. I attended a training session and knew it was for me. Drawn to get involved in something outside of myself, two weeks later, I was volunteering. Family Promise pulled me up and out of a painful place at a sorrowful time, aiding with the grieving process and helping me to heal.

I'm part of the team that prepares meals for families and welcomes them on Sundays—the first night of their stay in our church. I like working that night because it's often difficult for children to settle into a new place. As a retired educator, I relate well with the children and like entertaining them, especially since it helps give their parents a break after a stressful day.

A few times each week when we're hosting, I go to the church in the evening and offer to sit down with families as they're having dinner. I ask them, "Would you like some company?" Sometimes they're quiet, but often, they're okay with me joining them when they need to talk, and I'm a good listener and encourager.

I recall a single mother who had three small, hyperactive children. She seemed to be alone and somewhat overwhelmed. While other mothers stepped in to help with her kids, I took her outside for a break. The first thing I did was hug her. Then she asked me to pray with her. Afterward, we sat down and talked for a while. I learned she was ready to give up, but I assured her that with our help, I believed she could make it, and it wasn't the time to give up. Considering her children and what our organization could do, I encouraged her to stick with the program, and she did!

Having been with Family Promise for several years, I have asked myself, "Why am I so drawn to this?" I think it's because I have a brother three years older than me who was born with cerebral palsy and epilepsy. In those days, there wasn't any help for children with disabilities. My mother devoted herself to him 24-7. As a child, I felt incredible compassion coupled with the feeling of helplessness because I couldn't do anything to change his situation. However, I would have done anything to make life better for my brother. Sadly, I felt the same frustration when my husband was dying—the feeling of being there yet unable to fix it weighed heavily on me.

Volunteering in a program that has the potential to help change lives is empowering and an honor and a privilege. We provide hope that the children in these families and their children for generations to come will grow up with a better future.

Our goal is not just to give someone a place to sleep and something to eat. Families come to us with nowhere to go and no hope for the future. They feel that they don't matter. They're overwhelmed and discouraged. But entering a peaceful and calm environment where people care about them can change their perspective. They begin to see a way up and out and have a renewed sense of confidence that they can help themselves. We give families what they need physically and emotionally. If they're open to or need spiritual assistance, we offer that, too, but it's never pushed on them.

I deeply love our ministry, and knowing we can do something to help others is beautiful. Family Promise is a two-pronged ministry for families and volunteers because we never know what people are going through, including the volunteers. Sometimes we are healed too.

I am almost seventy-eight years old, and I look back upon my life in chapters. When my husband died, I turned the page and there was nothing written on it. Now, I'm writing furiously in this new phase of my life, which has exploded in many positive ways. I'm an introvert by nature, with a quiet, deep spirituality. I used to have only a few friends, but my network has changed. With my church affiliation and volunteer work, I've become outgoing. As a volunteer, I have benefitted greatly—I am a recipient of all the good Family Promise has done.

Thea's narrative underscores the invaluable role our volunteers play in the Family Promise mission. Their contributions are not only significant but often profoundly healing for them. After the heartbreaking loss of her husband, Dick, Thea found herself adrift, her sense of community and belonging eclipsed by the years she had committed to caring for her spouse. Volunteering furnished her with a newfound sense of connection and purpose. Thea's story of selfless giving, through which she embarked on her journey toward healing, underlines the transformative power of service for the beneficiaries and those who serve.

CHAPTER 14

Turning Enthusiasm into Action

Your calling is to be part of something bigger than yourself.

—Unknown

Having a desire to help others displays our concern for society as a whole. Whether shoveling snow for the elderly, grocery shopping for someone ill, collecting clothing for those in need, or making cookies or delicious treats for residents at a retirement home, when we feel drawn to contribute something, we should go for it. That altruistic urge to respond to a need we perceive is an adaptive response that I believe is a hardwired human instinct. There is no way our ancestors could have come this far as a civilization without bonding and forming communities whose members took care of one another.

Freely contributing our time and talents has benefits not only for the people we help but also for us. It can reduce stress and promote happiness because it gives us a sense of purpose and fulfillment to come up with creative solutions that uplift the people around us. Frankly, it is highly rewarding to express our talents, be it for bread baking or strategic planning.

For Burt Rothenburger, direct service to those in need inspired him to go further and further upstream in his endeavor to help house unhoused people. It all began three decades ago with his wife volunteering with Habitat for Humanity. She encouraged Burt to join her in meeting and cooking meals for some of the people who would move into the homes being built, as well as in building the houses. A manager of technical departments at Sunoco, Burt had the skills to organize the volunteers and quickly took on the job. When asked to join the charity's board, he saw that, with his business background, he could help them with the financial and governance issues that every nonprofit has to address. He was eager to get involved and generate solutions for as many people as he could.

BURT

One of the most moving experiences I've ever had was when I and other Habitat for Humanity volunteers went to a recently constructed home with a set of keys to turn over to the family. Their little boy, who was about eight years old, walked into what was going to be his room, and his eyes just lit up. He said, "I finally have my own room." I'll never forget it. I can still picture that little guy.

Homelessness in my area is considerable. Ours is the wealthiest county in Pennsylvania, but nonetheless, 27 percent of our households are still housing-cost burdened. That means that 27 percent of families are spending more than 30 percent of their income on housing.

When I timed off of the Habitat for Humanity board, I was looking around for something else to be involved with and joined the board of Family Service of Chester County, which provides free or low-cost counseling for individuals and families in need. After attending a briefing by Family Promise of Southern Chester County, I approached a senior pastor at my church and asked about putting up some unhoused families in the building temporarily. When my church agreed to help out, I had a model to approach other congregations, who also signed on. Soon, I became a primary recruiter of host congregations for the program.

I then became involved in the governance board of Chester County's program to end homelessness. We do a poverty simulation, and we train people to understand what the drivers are for people who are living in poverty. It also helps participants understand that impoverished people's goals, approaches to life, and daily management of their lives are entirely different from those of somebody like me. That piece is key. We've put everyone on our board through that training. In fact, I'm doing a poverty simulation a second time around.

As I've come to work with unhoused people, I've learned they can feel invisible. It's so important to recognize people, so I carry that over to other parts of my life. If I'm in a grocery store, I try to chat up the checkout clerk. I look for a name tag, and I say, "Hi, Marilyn. How are you doing today?" And I do the same thing with the grounds people. I chat with them. And I find that, in many cases, they just light up. They're not used to somebody doing that. And I have fun doing it.

I've also worked to educate advocates for affordable housing. The NIMBYs (not-in-my-backyarders) are rampant. There are a lot of supporters for affordable housing, but they don't know what to say. Part of our program to end homelessness is to create a group of people who will be advocates of affordable housing so that when the NIMBYs show up at a township meeting to try to defeat a zoning ordinance, we have a bunch of people who can speak for it.

I learned a lot from a group called FrameWorks Institute. They take controversial topics and do intensive research on how you get people who don't agree with each other to sit down and talk about these issues and seek common ground. About four years ago, they did a multiyear study on how to talk about affordable housing. Then they put together a playbook that explains that if you want to do it, here's what you should say and here's what you shouldn't say, and here are the approaches that work and here are the approaches that don't. We just "stole" that playbook.

In our area, we have Attainable Housing Councils, which have brought together elected officials, advocates, and developers to work together to change the way we do business in the area so we can promote affordable housing. Because of these collaborations, the councils have passed zoning ordinances that would remove restrictions to the development of accessory dwelling units (ADUs), sometimes called *in-law suites*, like an apartment over a garage, for example. Other changes in the works are permitting duplexes and triplexes in areas zoned for single-family homes.

Our church did a strategic-planning session about six years ago, and we came up with what we call four "God-sized dreams." One of these was to end homelessness and support affordable housing in our area. I was a coleader of that team. We have developed and are now rolling out an education package with videos and talking points on affordable housing advocacy. We are counting on the 450 faith communities we have here in our county to develop a strong group of advocates who can help turn this around.

As Burt has learned, working with others means helping them see how best to take their enthusiasm and turn it into action. His willingness to take a bird's-eye view of homelessness in his county has exponentially increased the number of families he's been able to assist.

Another volunteer, Cathy, had her keen sense of connectivity emerge at a strikingly young age. Just as an artist is innately tied to their paintbrush, Cathy discovered her intrinsic love—her need—for volunteering during her formative eighth-grade year. This youthful experience served as the awakening of a lifelong commitment, revealing to her that service to others was not merely an optional endeavor but an integral part of her being. When she's volunteering, Cathy is in her element and feels rewarded.

CATHY

Volunteer work has taught me how much we are all more alike, regardless of the way we look, how much money we have, our level of education, or our health. It seems to me all of us want peace, happiness, safety, a sense of being useful, people who love us, and people we can love.

Volunteer work has allowed me to get to know and respect people who have had very few opportunities in life in comparison to my own life. My first volunteer work introduced me to people in Appalachia who had very few resources. No indoor plumbing, not enough food, no car, and often no basic reading and writing skills. At a federal prison, I met people who were born to drug-addicted mothers and who lived their childhoods in dangerous and frightening families, schools, and neighborhoods.

While volunteering at a crisis hotline, I spoke with people who suffered from paralyzing mental-health problems and who saw self-harm as their only choice.

As a volunteer with Family Promise, I listened to guests who found themselves and their children living in cars or on the streets because they had no one to help them.

Working with all these different people convinced me that if I had their family circumstances, I myself could have easily lived a life in prison, on the streets, or in constant despair. Throughout my volunteer experiences helping those less fortunate, the generosity, kindness, gratitude, and dignity from them have been noteworthy, despite their tragic lives. Following Hurricane Katrina, for example, I have the vivid memory of residents in Louisiana neighborhoods, totally demolished by the storm, offering to accept only one Red Cross meal for their whole family "so that there's enough food for our neighbors too."

People I met while volunteering inspired me, expanded my understanding of real-life struggles, increased my gratitude for the many opportunities I've had in my life, and often delighted me with their senses of humor in spite of very harsh settings. Volunteering, for me, has always been both meaningful and enjoyable. I believe I have always received more than I was able to give. It is a privilege to be allowed to be a part of the lives of those I meet in volunteer work. They have taught me truly important lessons, and their willingness to allow me into their lives is always humbling.

In addition, it has been a real pleasure to work with many other wonderful volunteers. I love volunteers! My most significant friendships all have roots in volunteer work or work within a faith community. These friendships span over fifty years, and in all cases, these friends continue to volunteer in their communities today. They inspire me and give me much hope for our world.

———

I spoke with Marc, a semiretired private-equity professional in his sixties, shortly after the anniversary of his third year serving as a mentor to seventeen-year-old Abraham through Big Brothers Big Sisters of Orange County, California. Their match has been so successful that Marc was asked to mentor other mentors coming into the program, to encourage them and act as a role model. He has tried to be an ambassador for the program and enlist other folks like himself who have time, passion, and financial means to give of themselves to youth. His experience with Abe has enriched his life to such a degree that he plans to jump back in with a second Little Brother after Abe graduates from the program.

MARC

It blows me away that more people don't want to do this. Being Abe's Big Brother has given me more than I ever could give back. It really has. I grew up in Huntington Beach in an Anglo, upper-middle-class neighborhood. The community was so White that, for example, there was only one Black kid in the high school of 4,000 students. Abe is Hispanic and lives in a 700-square-foot one-bedroom apartment with his mom, who cleans houses and offices to make a living about fifteen miles away. He has never met his father, who lives in Mexico. What I didn't bargain for, or expect, was that I was going to receive life lessons and joy by becoming a benefactor to somebody of a different race and generation. Having Abe as my Little has given me experiences, knowledge, and insights into myself that are invaluable.

We initiated this experience right in the middle of COVID. That was challenging and awkward. I spent nine months getting to know him on Zoom calls. There weren't a lot of people to go to for recommendations on how to go about this, so I just saddled up. We would talk once a week about his school and his social interactions, and I did my best to offer tutelage. When we finally met face to face, however, our relationship blossomed.

I love to brag about what a life-changing experience it is to be involved in a teenager's life. It's probably even more so for me than for some because I never had kids of my own, or wanted them, if I'm being honest, because I was always looking for the next promotion, the next big house, the next trip. This calling for me is my opportunity to experience having a teenager. It's like a different universe. Before Big Brothers, I'd checked out volunteer opportunities at the local YMCA. Because I played basketball and baseball in high school and college, they asked me to coach intramural sports. But for kids that didn't have a worry in the world. Instead, I made a call to Big Brothers and after a background check, training, and some interviews, they paired me with Abe.

If I had to sum up the experience in a sentence, I'd say it has been eye-opening to learn how other people struggle, how they live, how they survive, the things they take pride in, the things that bring them joy. I love taking Abe to do things he's never done before. He had never played miniature golf. He'd never played basketball. He'd never been go-kart racing or flown a kite. Simple activities I'd been blessed to do as a kid enriched his life.

But our connection is not all about entertainment. We sit down and pour over his report card, going line item by line item, having a discussion on each subject. He's a good student, and he understands the importance of keeping his GPA up. We talk about goals and objectives. Abe has a job working at a trampoline park, where he earns $19 an hour. We set up a bank account for him with checking and a debit card, and developed a budget. I taught him how to work with the calendar and to-do list on his phone but also to work with a written planner on paper. He's hungry for knowledge.

He also asked me to work with him on his manners and etiquette. He wants to know how to be a respectful adult in our society. When he asked me how he could stand apart from his peers, I made him personalized stationery with his initials on it and envelopes with his name and address, so he could write thank-you notes when he was grateful for something nice someone had done for him, like when his girlfriend's parents took him out for dinner. To show his appreciation.

Abe is in his senior year of high school, and he has decisions to make about his future. He's at an interesting crossroads. He's more drawn to attending a vocational school to learn how to be an electrician than to a four-year college. One of his uncles is a painter and another is a plumber. He is impressed by their work ethic, their diligence in finishing projects and doing them right. That he is bilingual can be an advantage for him in being in a trade. We visited a trade school together. The expense of nine months of education—which includes two days a week on campus, five hours a day, then ten to fourteen hours of lab work on a computer—even after a Pell grant, which he would qualify for, is $10,000. He doesn't have it. Nor does his mom. Fortunately, I put together a fund for him at the beginning to help him through whatever educational path he decides to take. We're working with a career specialist to identify the right opportunity for a young man like Abe. It may be a two-year junior college.

Not everyone is going to create a Facebook like Mark Zuckerberg or a Tesla like Elon Musk. But there will always be a need for plumbers, electricians, welders, and mechanics; and in those careers, Abe could climb the financial ladder fairly quickly. Still, it would take commitment and effort and schooling to realize those gains. As a mentor and a guide, I can't just put down my foot like my dad did for me and force Abe to go to college. I let him know I could help him get on course, but that the financial support I am offering is a one-shot deal. Even so, he'll be in my life forever. Period. I've told him so.

Some people fear retirement because they can't imagine what they're going to do. Not me. I'm a big believer in having different buckets of activities in your life. A reading bucket. A meditation bucket. A give-back bucket. My parents were both givers. My mom did missionary service in a women's prison, and it was moving at her funeral when 250 people showed up to pay respects for her contribution to turning their lives around. It was such a tribute. My wife works philanthropically with cancer survivors in her art studio making art. Before I found Big Brothers, I had a nagging need to give back. I just hadn't discovered my niche yet.

This experience with Abraham has been amazing for how it put me out there. There's no place to hide. It's you, and you're learning as you go. You have to be creative and come up with the right ingredients to make the best "cake" you can make. The more ingredients the better.

———

Many people these days often think that happiness comes from buying the latest gadget or posting images on Instagram or Facebook to show off a luxurious vacation they took. But if you reach beyond yourself to others, happiness actually catches up with you. It is a pleasure to be around people that care for you and with whom you feel safe. Human bonding and social connection are significant sources of genuine joy and fulfillment.

CHAPTER 15

We Are All Connected

Kindness is the golden chain by which society
is bound together.
—Johann Wolfgang von Goethe

One of the strongest reasons why doing good is so good for us is that we are all connected, and doing good aligns us more closely with the rest of humanity. Spiritual leaders have been talking about our interconnectedness for as long as anyone can remember. Physicists have even joined in on the conversation, noting that 99.9 percent of all matter in the observable universe is made up of exactly the same thing. When we have that much in common with a distant star, how can we possibly not feel connected to the people whose paths we cross every single day?

There is much more common ground in most religious ideologies than what might appear on the surface or what we have been led to believe. I knew the only way to make Family Promise work was if I had the cooperation and connection of congregations of all faiths working together. At the core, every religion believes its mission is to help those less fortunate, so we were successful in pulling together churches, synagogues, and mosques around one common objective: faith and service to others.

One of the things I often hear from people is that they would love to do something to improve the lives of others. But they never get started because they don't feel they can make any appreciable difference. However, I have learned that even the smallest act of kindness can have a substantial positive effect.

The ten minutes you take to help a student understand a math problem can help boost their confidence in a subject they might be struggling in. Working at an animal shelter adoption drive could save a puppy's life. The time you give to improve a family's life can give them hope and cause them to willingly do the same for others. *Any* little act of kindness can resonate with someone in a way that may be unimaginable to you.

Chuck, a Family Promise volunteer, was meeting Rebecca, a homeless mother, at 5:00 a.m. to pick her up, because she couldn't drive due to car trouble. At first, he made a commitment to help for a few days, but then he continued to do so for three weeks. Then, one morning, on his way to meet her, Chuck made a detour.

CHUCK

I stopped and got Rebecca a latte because she mentioned she liked them. Then, I stood outside waiting for her with my coffee in one hand and her latte in the other until she arrived. When she came out and saw me, she was taken aback by my kindness as I handed her the latte.

Her eyes welled as she confessed, "Chuck, you're going to make me cry," and she did. Rebecca told me I'd made what had been an especially rough stretch for her so much more bearable. I could see how much a simple and warm act of kindness had touched her deeply. Small acts of kindness can have an astounding ripple effect and, in many ways, bring us closer as a community. They are not to be taken for granted.

"A day like any other at Covenant House? That doesn't exist. No day is like the other," Nabijah Shabazz said to me, laughing as she confessed, "I love working with young people. And I love that I can make a difference in someone's life."

Nabijah is the volunteer coordinator at Covenant House, which helps homeless children and those who have gotten away from human trafficking by providing shelter and support. She has been making a difference in the lives of children for over six years, proving that the more we help people, the stronger our connection with them becomes.

For youth in need, coming to Covenant House means being around peers and other young people with similar backgrounds. And there are various reasons for them to seek help there. The relationship Nabijah has with the youth at Covenant House is like a tapestry. Each thread is unique, but together they create a beautiful, strong piece of art.

NABIJAH

No story is the same, no youth is the same. I want them to feel accepted from the moment they come to us at Covenant House. I love that even during the pandemic, people contacted me, asking how they could support us. I am grateful my path led me there.

A few years back, a young man came in. While we were chatting, he told me he'd never had a birthday party in his whole life. I couldn't believe it—this poor kid! But I will never forget his face when he returned a few days later, and we surprised him by throwing him a party. These are moments I cherish deeply. Today, we have a whole group of volunteers in charge of celebrations. By showing love and support to young people and accepting them the way they are without judgment, we are helping them regain their life and self-respect. Isn't that what it should all be about? As we help others, we also help ourselves grow, heal, and strive to be our best.

We have volunteers teaching financial literacy skills to help the youths keep track of their budgets once they've moved into their own apartments. While at Covenant House, they can begin to heal, aspire to do more, and ultimately do better. Many young people are eager to return to high school to achieve their diploma or GED, and some want to pursue college—which is progress!

In an unexpected turn of events, Sandra Rolling, a middle school teacher from Newark, New Jersey, found her path to volunteering at Covenant House. Sandra happened upon a newspaper interview about the organization's Sleep Out initiatives, which resembled a similar endeavor at her church. This serendipitous discovery sparked her curiosity about how she could involve herself in their mission. Thus, Sandra found her path to becoming a dedicated volunteer for Covenant House.

SANDRA

I love reading and have facilitated a book club for our middle school students for years. Additionally, I'm part of the ReadUP Book Club, a subsidiary of United Way, and I tutor children at the Family Success Center in East Orange, New Jersey. So, I reached out to Nabijah, the volunteer coordinator at Covenant House. She hit the nail on the head when proposing I run a book club for them.

Besides working as a full-time teacher and volunteering, I support different organizations and help in food and soup kitchens. But none of that feels like working at Covenant House. It's almost like coming home! When I get there after a long day at school, it's just different. I walk in and can see someone's passion and love for reading and how much they enjoy it, and I recognize we share the same passion. So, I purposely adapted the book club to accommodate the young people participating. I made copies of short stories that would resonate with them, and we now have a whole collection. Everyone who shows up receives a copy, and we read it together and then talk about it.

I participate in one of our biggest fundraisers for Covenant House, which is an annual sleep out, held in a parking lot in

Newark, New Jersey, called "Night of the Stars." Though it's cold and scary, the sleep outs are incredibly special. We want to stand in solidarity with the kids and understand what they must endure. It sets precedence and is symbolic because the kids sleep inside while we spend the night outside. It's a convenient inconvenience, because we can sleep outdoors but still go back inside to our regular lives. Homeless people don't have that luxury. They're out there sleeping wherever they find shelter.

Volunteering is my way of giving back. Despite not having a wealthy upbringing, God blessed me, and I was raised to be grateful for what I have. In the end, what matters is the compassion we have for someone else. We're all connected. You can't look helplessly at someone struggling and not do something about it. When I give back, I feel like that's the service I pay for and the privilege I get for living on this Earth: I enjoy it—a lot!

A recent study has shown that people witnessing others performing kind acts leads to a state of elevation that increases our desire to help others. Who wouldn't want to feel good like that?

Think about what a small, considerate act can do. Hold a door for someone, smile at a stranger, write a get-well card, or offer to share an umbrella with a stranger getting wet on the street corner. It helps people and is likely to cause others to act similarly, spreading goodwill even further.

Compassion is an endlessly renewable resource with an

unlimited supply. It costs us nothing to give, and it benefits us. In addition, research indicates we feel a heightened sense of happiness when we act out of compassion; it's a natural response to the realization that we are all interconnected.

CHAPTER 16

The Warmth of a Smile

Out of difficulties grow miracles.

—Jean de la Bruyère

Yusuf, Jane, and their young daughter, Jobiah, bravely decided to leave their home in Uganda and seek a better life in the United States, with just $4 and a few clothes to their name. Their journey wasn't easy, but they embarked on this new chapter in their lives with determination and hope. When their friend in Framingham, Massachusetts, who had initially welcomed them into his apartment, notified them that they could no longer stay, Yusuf and Jane found themselves facing homelessness in an unfamiliar country, not knowing where to turn.

YUSUF

Initially, I planned on coming to the United States alone and sending for my wife and daughter after I was settled, but we participated in a green-card lottery, and due to some administrative issues at the embassy, we were told that if I went to America, my family had to go at the same time. We accepted the opportunity.

When we arrived in the States, I didn't know anyone other than my friend. Having brought my wife, Jane, and daughter, Jobiah, I had no money and only a few options. Trying to help, my friend took me downtown to a food pantry in Framingham. I noticed people smiling generously while giving us free food and graciously offering to carry it to my car—only I didn't own one.

On the two-mile walk back to my temporary home, I thought about the people who had been serving us. I'd been surprised to learn they were all volunteers. Seeing their passion for helping people in need made me forget about my situation, and like them, I smiled. Incredibly moved by what they were doing, I returned, but it was to volunteer, and I was happy to join their team. Besides, I didn't have anything else to offer other than my time. Every morning at the pantry, I went and put food together and served people lunch. It gave me another purpose while trying to create a new life.

Sometimes, when we're in a bad situation, we think no one has been through what we're experiencing, and no one understands us. But I realized that by getting out and talking with people, my family would be introduced to new opportunities. I knew that through my service, regardless of my circumstances, I was the reason for a smile on someone's face.

I spoke with a few volunteers and told them I needed to find a place to live. Then, someone told me about Family Promise, so I asked my friend if he knew anything about them. He explained that they help people who are homeless by offering shelter in several of the local churches. After talking to the executive director over the phone, I received a call from a case manager who offered to send a van to pick up my family and me. Instantly, I was filled with hope.

When we arrived, I knocked on the door, and the executive director opened it, smiling as if she knew me. The warmth of a smile is something everyone understands. After I filled out some paperwork, we went to the church, and although I didn't know anyone, it wasn't uncomfortable.

The volunteers had just prepared lasagna for dinner and graciously invited us to join them. We had never eaten any of the foods they'd prepared before, and a woman noticed we weren't familiar with the dishes and asked where we were from; I told her central Uganda. To our pleasant surprise, the following night's dinner they served to us was a Ugandan meal of rice and beans. It touched our hearts that someone went out of their way to make us feel more comfortable and at home. The volunteers and other guests were welcoming, and there was no judgment. Everyone smiled as though they were happy to meet and accommodate us. When dinner was over, one of them took us to our room, which was decorated with beautiful, welcoming messages.

I was overwhelmed because, where I come from, people don't talk to anyone the way they do at Family Promise. I wasn't from a background where I was loved. I was isolated, and we didn't have anything. Although those feelings resurfaced, I was grateful to be in a welcoming, albeit foreign, environment with my family. What struck me was the attitude of the volunteers. From their tone of voice, eye contact, and communication, I could tell they weren't there to do a job. Instead, they were there because they cared and wanted to help. And I realized that if they were there to help us, we must be ready to be helped.

The following morning, I asked one of the volunteers if they could drop me off at the local mall. I knew there were hundreds of shops, and I could look for a job. I accepted an offer to work at Macy's, where I learned how to operate a credit-card machine, use the register, and help shoppers.

Family Promise wanted to help our family and noticed that my wife needed more skills, so they helped her go to school to become a Certified Nursing Assistant. I found it even more encouraging that they supported both of us working and helped pay for Jobiah's daycare. Everything was done with kindness, and in the same language—with a smile.

When we were without a home or a place to stay, the people I talked to were angels sent to me. A few people even asked what type of job I wanted so they could help me match my skills. In Uganda, I had worked with a consultancy firm training workers in customer service, business development, and communications, and I taught these skills at a technical institute. Hearing about this background, one of the volunteers gave me his business card and told me to send him my resume. When I read his card, I learned that this gentleman was the board chairman of a nonprofit organization called Lutheran Social Services. Cara at Family Promise was a human resources expert who kindly helped me with my resume.

I was hired as an administrative assistant at the corporate headquarters of Lutheran Social Services, occasionally traveling to a field office. The position at Lutheran Social Services increased my income from $9 an hour to $15. The only problem was that I still didn't have a car. But I had incredibly supportive friends who drove me to work, and one of them bought a used car for $3,000 and generously gave it to me. Then, with complete trust, he told me, "When you get the money, you can pay me back."

Working equally as hard to help improve our situation, Jane got a part-time job at Dunkin' Donuts while attending school. The additional income helped. We worked hard and saved everything possible while staying in the Family Promise program for nine months. We moved into transitional housing, and after a year, we were able to stand on our own feet.

With the help of Family Promise, we moved into an affordable apartment. But, still saving money, we didn't own much. Family Promise circulated an email to garner further assistance for us, and without hesitation, people responded, asking us what we needed. It was humbling, and I don't know if they understood the impact it had on us. Although I volunteer, what was created on such a large scale made me wonder how they unite all these people with the same passion and shared goals to serve. I have prayed that I'll stop being on the receiving side and instead be on the giving side, and it's coming to pass.

In addition to volunteering at Family Promise, I work as a credentialing specialist at St. Vincent Hospital when I have time. And I have a night job as a home caregiver at Home Instead Senior Care, an agency that helps veterans and the elderly.

Family Promise helped me lay the foundation in this new country. I've maintained relationships with some volunteers, and we've become friends. I am proud to speak to congregations about my history when I can. Through the kindness and compassion of others, I've been able to turn despair into hope and discouragement into a fresh start. I want all the volunteers and people in these religious congregations to look at me and see the fruits of their giving, generosity, and compassion.

Yusuf's story underscores the importance of how volunteers make a difference in the lives of others, whether with a light touch or something more substantial. While some may view his progress and achievements as unattainable, it is important to recognize that anything is possible with the right resources and a helping hand. Yusuf's gratitude toward the volunteers and the community that supported him is palpable. He acknowledges that their generosity and willingness to lend a hand were instrumental in helping him achieve stability and overcome homelessness. His belief that volunteers are the backbone of organizations like Family Promise is a testament to the importance of volunteerism and its critical role in building stronger, more resilient communities.

For Yusuf, volunteering is not just a way to give back but also a means of fighting homelessness and helping others on their journey toward stability. His story highlights the ripple effect of kindness and support, as the impact of those who helped him extends beyond his own experience to inspire him to give back and pay it forward.

CHAPTER 17

Sadie's North Star

> Do your little bit of good where you are; it's those little bits of good put together that overwhelm the world.
>
> —Desmond Tutu

The impact of the work done by the Family Promise community is so significant that it can be difficult to fully comprehend. After my speeches, attendees often ask, "Did you have any idea what you were creating and the impact it would have?" It's hard for me to get my heart and mind around what has been established, because we have changed the lives of so many families and volunteers. Through our program, families have gained renewed confidence, support, and trust, knowing they have a community of caring individuals behind them. Our volunteers truly are a gift that keeps on giving.

Despite her difficulties, including a dark past, Sadie Johnson found hope and a new beginning through our program. She reflects on New Year's Day 2019 as both the worst day of her life and the best day, as it marked the turning point toward a brighter future. Sadie's story highlights the power of compassion and how it can transform lives, even in the face of adversity.

On a cold morning in southern Chester, Pennsylvania, Sadie was living in a small rental home, one of many designed for survivors of domestic violence. Her son, Silas, almost four, was with her, as was another woman and her children, who were in similar circumstances and awaiting housing.

At about 8:00 a.m., as Sadie and Silas slept, Sadie's abusive boyfriend—her son's father—had coaxed the other woman into letting him into the house, and he was armed. He loaded his gun with a red laser on it, and then, for two long hours, held her hostage with the gun to her head. I listened as Sadie courageously recalled her experience.

SADIE

My ex-boyfriend, Todd, had already been issued a Protection From Abuse notice, but nothing would stop him. On New Year's Day, with mounting rage, he ripped me out of bed, snatched my phone, and relentlessly questioned and berated me. When Todd didn't hear what he needed, he threatened me with his gun—even with our son there. Without another option, I had to fight back, so I tried wrestling the gun away, but he bashed my head into the hard edge of my couch at least twenty times. I was in a mode where I thought I'd have to kill him because I feared that one of us would die. It would probably be me, but then I thought about my son, Silas. Who would protect him?

I didn't know it then, but I had suffered a terrible concussion. I forged on because I was afraid for Silas. It was up to me to protect him. I tried to divert Todd's attention to defuse the situation. He didn't get along with my mom, who he knew could be very persistent and consistent when we had plans. Todd knew that, so I pretended my mom was expecting me, I asked him what time it was, and I told him I needed to use the phone to call my mom and tell her I wasn't going to her house. I told him she would come to the house where I was staying if I didn't show up.

Todd took the bait and let me use the phone. When I told Mom I wouldn't be able to make it, she knew immediately something was amiss, because we didn't actually have any plans to see each other. Sensing something was wrong, Mom asked if Todd was there, and I indicated yes. Mom said she would be there in ten minutes, and she immediately called the police and explained everything to them. When she arrived at the house, Todd dashed upstairs to hide the gun, and I ran Silas outside and locked him inside Mom's car. The police arrived just in time. When they searched the house, they found the loaded gun wrapped in a sweatshirt and hidden in my closet. Todd was sentenced to time in prison.

I was transported to the hospital and treated for a concussion. It was so bad that the doctor told me I couldn't return to work. Although it wasn't my fault, my landlord ended my lease because of the violence at the house that day. Against my physician's advice, I got a job as a waitress. I was strapped for money and doing my darndest to make ends meet, but despite my best efforts, Silas and I were about to become homeless. Completely lost, I didn't know where to turn, so I went to Connect Points, a counseling and human service agency, where a wonderful person, Anthony, pointed me to Family Promise.

Naturally, I had a great deal of trepidation entering Family Promise with my son, but my caseworker, Omar Hernandez, put my mind at ease. Omar helped me see things about myself and my situation that I hadn't considered. Rather than talking about what was wrong, he helped me create a plan for overcoming my circumstances. He never made me feel my situation was bigger than what I could overcome, which filled me with hope. Throughout the entire process, Omar was amazing. And in the grand scheme of things, all the team members in all the congregations were kindhearted, open armed, and willing to help. They didn't pity me or allow me to feel sorry for myself; instead, they gave me what I needed. Family Promise was my North Star. I followed their path and trusted the program that had helped thousands of others.

It was all love. The people serving us a hot meal were happy. We had a roof over our heads, a bed to sleep in, food to eat, and people to go to for support. I never felt animosity or judgment. It was the most rewarding experience ever, and I'm proud of the lessons I learned there. I've grown in a way where I'm not ashamed to tell anybody I was in a homeless shelter, because it brought so much peace to my heart. Experiencing homelessness taught me to humble myself and be grateful for all I have. Getting into the program and receiving help throughout the entire process was tremendous.

When Silas and I first entered Family Promise, I felt despair, defeat, and numbness over my situation. But the program's structure got me through those challenging times, including the early wake up, chores, and paperwork I did while searching for jobs and potential places to live. I loved it because it kept me accountable for my actions and what I had to do.

Like many Family Promise guests, Sadie learned that her past did not have to define her future or who she was; but it could be embraced. Sadie explained, "I own that part of my story, and no one can take it away. If you utilize everything you have—the opportunities, the people, and the help—you can literally walk out of your program in such a positive space, and they're forever your family."

Sadie landed a job as a dental assistant working forty hours a week while with us. She told her son, Silas, to consider their experience with our organization like it was a camping adventure. Since Sadie was beginning to work more hours, the team at Family Promise pitched in and cared for Silas for a good part of each day, feeding, bathing, and encouraging him, so he would never feel alone or unloved.

With humility, Sadie confessed, "I'm so thankful. It makes me want to cry. Everything happens for a reason. I'll always be grateful for everything they've done for me. I don't think I truly understood unconditional love until experiencing homelessness. To have people go out of their way to ensure you're comfortable, loved, recognized, appreciated, and uplifted—we established a bond I will forever hold dear."

Sadie and Silas eventually moved into their own home, and she landed her dream job as a full-time business coordinator at a neighboring dental clinic. She remains heavily involved with Family Promise and continues to volunteer.

CHAPTER 18

The Ripple Effect

I alone cannot change the world, but I can cast a stone across the waters to create many ripples.

—Mother Teresa

Giving our time, compassion, and support to others can create a ripple effect. When someone witnesses an act of kindness, they are more likely to show kindness to others too. Watching a video showing an act of kindness or letting someone enter a roadway first at a four-way stop sign may seem trivial, but each choice of doing something kind can have far-reaching effects. Every day, everyone has a chance to influence our world, and what better way than to pass on kindness.

There are many ways we can help, leaving much to choose from that will tug on our heartstrings and even encourage others to join in. Your journey may lead you to make an incredible impact by becoming a mentor; volunteering for disaster relief; supporting senior groups; serving at a community shelter or soup kitchen; or working at a food bank, a church, a hospital, an environmental organization, or even an animal shelter. Kindness knows no boundaries! If you think you have little to offer, remember that no commitment is too little, as it's often more appreciated than you know. Even spontaneous acts of kindness matter. They are uplifting and impactful and can change lives and restore faith in humanity.

Once when I was away from home, it snowed. My neighbor, Chris Jordan, shoveled my driveway and walkway and left a beautiful note on my door, saying, "I knew you were away. I hope I didn't ruin anything. I shoveled your driveway and sidewalk." His kindness meant so much to me that I saved Chris's note. Picturing the time Chris spent in my driveway in the cold, braving the elements, all to help me out warmed my soul. Do what moves you, or do something you would want someone to do for you. Collect the packages piling up on your neighbor's porch until they return, offer to pick up something from the grocery store for an elderly neighbor, or just check in on someone who may be alone and offer to spend time with them. *Compassion breeds gratitude,* so let's create an incredible ripple effect by showing kindness to others.

Natural disasters such as hurricanes, wildfires in California and Canada, tornadoes in the Midwest, and flooding, coupled with forced migration, have rallied individuals and organizations to collectively offer assistance to those affected. COVID and its variants added another threat for families who lost their jobs and then their homes. Even though stimulus checks were given by the government, many argued it wasn't enough support.

Seeing a need is a call to get involved, whether it's tutoring a child, cooking a meal for someone who is struggling, or donating canned goods to a food pantry. It's about putting your compassion into action.

Because we at Family Promise identified the need of family homelessness, one of the beautiful things we accomplished was creating an environment suitable for families. All the guests I interviewed for this book expressed that when they came to Family Promise and the volunteers approached them, they finally felt someone cared about them. Many of the guests can gladly recall the names and faces of the volunteers who helped them because they were never treated as strangers. Reciprocally, the gift of caring is continually returned, as many of our guests find ways to continue supporting the well-being and success of others through Family Promise, other organizations, or on their own.

―

On October 1, 2017, Tom was working as a private security guard at the Route 91 Harvest music festival in Las Vegas, Nevada, when the largest mass shooting in U.S. history took place. He was positioned next to the stage when the shooting began. This tragic event left a lasting impact on Tom and thousands of others, many of whom struggled to cope with the trauma and found themselves living in isolation or fear.

Tom made the decision to leave Las Vegas to ensure a safer environment for his young daughter. They embarked on a road trip over spring break to start the process of finding a new town to live in across various states, but unfortunately, their car broke down in Maryville, Tennessee.

During this unexpected stop, Tom contacted his landlord in Las Vegas to let him know they would be in Tennessee for a bit longer, as they tried to figure out what he would do about his car. The landlord informed Tom that they didn't need to hurry back because the apartment complex they lived in had burned down while they were gone. Nothing was left of their belongings, and now everything they owned was in the suitcase they had packed for a weeklong vacation. Just like that, everything was lost.

With nowhere else to go, Tom and his daughter were forced to live in their car for two weeks until they discovered our organization.

TOM

Since my daughter and I were in the Family Promise program a few years ago, life has gradually improved. We went through the shelter program, transitional housing, and finally into permanent housing, where we've been for two and a half years. I've remained in contact with Family Promise because they are such an amazing organization that helped us when we needed it most and were on our road to healing.

Our experience inspired me to give back to the community in some way. As a mechanic, I find it fulfilling to take something broken and make it whole again. I saw there were gaps in services offered to those experiencing homelessness that could be addressed. After my experience with Family Promise, I started a nonprofit food ministry called the Longer Table. When I presented the idea to my church, they were hesitant, because they weren't sure if it was needed. I made it very clear to them there was a need, relaying firsthand experience about when my daughter and I would go with no meals from Thursday night to Monday morning because there weren't any hot-food pantries open on Fridays or over the weekends. Too often, people put up taller fences that prevent them from seeing the problems around them. I was sure they were compassionate Christians and would see that we must build a longer table, not a taller fence.

When we host a meal, we will set up our dining room with long tables in a gym to encourage people to connect. We want to feed people physically, but also spiritually. Many of my volunteers serve our guests and then sit down to share a meal with them. Seeing people engage in conversation for an hour or more is heartwarming. We have forty-five volunteers from ten to ninety years old who show up weekly. They know the guests by name and are invested in their lives. I want to help people realize that those who need help are just like us, and we're all the same. It's beautiful to see that when they leave, everybody is spiritually uplifted and encouraged.

My goal with the Longer Table is to open people's eyes to the reality that one in three working families in our county is food insecure, which is a considerable number. The situation here differs from that of a big city; thankfully, there aren't as many people sleeping on the streets. Nonetheless, some are really struggling, and it's important to help them in any way we can. That is not where their road ends. If nothing else, through kindness and a meal, we can encourage people to take the road to healing.

After experiencing support from the Maryville community during a time of need, Tom felt an internal desire to reciprocate their kindness. His story is an example of how the act of giving back not only benefits the recipients but also enriches the giver's own life and fosters a sense of purpose. By engaging in service to others, individuals can gain a deeper understanding of their community and its needs, promoting emotional well-being and personal growth. Additionally, compassion can facilitate helping others take the road to healing, providing a forum for mutual understanding and compassion.

The perspective of volunteers is so informative. It's important to know what volunteers are getting out of their time spent in an organization and why they keep at it.

At age twenty-four, with her life in good order and her finances stable, Deborah Jackson started as a mentor to eight-year-old Jessica Walters through Big Brothers Big Sisters (BBBS) of Greater Cleveland because she wanted to give back in some way. Becoming a Big was the first volunteer experience she ever had. After researching different opportunities and asking the question "Where could I truly be of most benefit?" this role spoke most to her.

Deborah wanted to make a significant impact on the life of a child, which she believed would happen only by being a stable, consistent presence. Three decades later, she and Jessica are still in each other's lives and regard one another as family. Her impact and the ripple effect of her volunteerism as a Big Sister cannot be denied. Deborah's Little Sister, Jessica Walters, is now thirty-seven years old and currently president and CEO of BBBS of Greater Cleveland, a position she's held for the last five years.

DEBORAH

I became aware of Big Brothers Big Sisters through an advertising campaign running on TV. My impulse to sign up for this came from feeling I had "extra" to share. I was living on my own. I had a corporate job in marketing. I was dating, but I had no immediate plans to be married or have my own children. After doing a deep dive into research, I concluded that many of the problems in our society are systemic—and if you help somebody only once, they're likely going to need help again a day or two later. But if you can help an individual change within themself, change more than their circumstances, then you've made a serious, lasting impact. In my mind, it's like the old saying, "Teach a man to fish, and he can feed himself for the rest of his life." I wanted my time to matter, so I volunteered to mentor a Little.

There was a process involved in being approved and then getting a match. BBBS did a background check and several interviews. They asked my preferences in regard to race, religion, and hobbies. Girls are matched with women and boys with men. I left everything open, and yet we were well matched from the beginning. Jessica is the second oldest of four children. Her mom, Mary Ellen, had to sign her up. She was divorced, working full-time as a nurse, and just overwhelmed. The dad was not around much. Kudos to Mary Ellen for reaching out, as it is not easy for parents to say, "Hey, I need help."

There is a caseworker involved in every match. The program has changed over the years, but back then, the commitment was to speak to the Little on the phone once a week and get together once a week for a full day. BBBS would loosen the commitment after a few years—once the relationship was well established. As a Big, I had to speak to the caseworker and then the parent before getting on the phone with my Little. There were no overnights, and we rarely hung out at my apartment, though we did occasionally stay in and play board games. Although I was told, "You just need to be a friend and spend time with the Little," I wanted to be intentional about everything we did. Without pushing Jessica toward any one thing, my aim was to show her there was a lot going on out in the world. That people live in different ways and have different cultures.

I wanted the best for Jessica. And to me, the best starts with knowing, on some level, that you have autonomy and options. Choices about what you do. You aren't limited to taking a job that's around the corner because that's all you've ever seen. If you can dream it and imagine it, then it's possible for you. The whole world is there for you, not just for other people. We did cultural things, went to plays and art galleries in downtown Cleveland. If there was a museum to be seen, we went to it.

The limitations in Jessica's household weren't purely due to a lack of financial resources. There was disorder at home. Jessica knew she was loved but she was basically parenting herself and her siblings. The house was in disrepair, and I never knew what I was going to find when I showed up. She would be wearing old, dirty clothes all the time. I had to set boundaries for myself to prioritize Jessica and not start trying to fix the whole household. Without that, it would have been an endless task. Even so, it was difficult for me. I knew and cared about the other three kids. Interestingly, Jessica was protective of me. I was hers. We only invited another child along with us a handful of times—and only after several years.

I remember the first time we met. I was working in the corporate world and had on a suit, a skirt, and heels, which is funny to me, since I don't go anywhere like that anymore. I came to her house, and we sat in the living room. I made sure to come down to her eye level. Remember, she was eight. It was awkward, since I was a stranger, but I tried to be as casual as possible. What broke the ice was that I spoke with her mother for a bit in her presence before we talked alone. Then I pulled out a printout of suggested outings the organization had given me and asked, "Is there anything here you'd be particularly interested in doing? Something that seems exciting?" We checked off a few things, such as ice-skating. Everything from taking walks in the park to horseback riding was on the list. Going forward, we started checking them off.

Intentionally, I didn't shower Jessica with material things. Certainly, I would pay entry fees to go someplace, but the majority of the time, we would do things that did not cost money. The only time I would buy her things was for a birthday or Christmas. My primary goal was to develop our relationship, and I felt it would be counterproductive if she saw me as a means to get stuff she needed or wanted. I hoped she would begin to view me as a personal resource for wisdom and life experience, and a source of security and emotional stability. I didn't want the other kids to covet goodies she might have gotten because they felt envious.

Ninety-five percent of the time, Jessica and I would not speak about her household or life with her siblings and mom. Mostly, we would talk about the place where we were. I would teach her about the context. If we were at an art museum, I would explain that it was free because it was funded by donations. Some people gave $5, and some gave a million.

I wanted her to know how the world works. She wasn't a chatterbox, so it was like pulling teeth sometimes to get her to open up, but she told me she had a dream of living in a house on a hill someday and loved the idea of riding horses.

I did a lot of firsts with Jess: ice-skating, cross-country skiing, and riding in a plane for her first time. The organization had a partnership with Delta Airlines, so we flew from Cleveland to Detroit. We took a tour of the airline cafeteria and learned how they prepare food for the planes. Then we got back on a plane and came home. That was a great outing. She was a little nervous, but happy.

I always made a point to get her a cake for her birthday, because she never had a party at home. Also, during the holidays we would drive around to see Christmas lights and decorations, or we would attend a Christmas play to do something festive together so she would see she had a choice to be in the Christmas spirit.

She came with me to Take Your Daughter to Work Day at my office. This had quite an impact on her, seeing me in a different environment. Seeing a woman having her own office, commanding some authority over a budget, attending a meeting. This expanded her horizons. I attended both her high school and college graduations. I'm not sure she would have gone to college without support from BBBS. For my part, at every age and stage, I focused on the step she was taking then. When she was a teenager, I hoped she wouldn't get pregnant or do drugs. I hoped she wouldn't get a criminal record. I tried to help her move in positive directions, to get into college, then to finish college. Not by pressuring her, but through an organic process.

Looking back, my friendship with Jessica is a precious

relationship that has absolutely enriched my life. I feel such a sense of satisfaction and joy from knowing her as a person and watching her grow. She applied and got into Case Western Reserve University, and I helped her move into her dorm. When she was eighteen, she graduated from the mentorship program, and we mutually decided we wanted to stay connected. I hosted a bridal shower for her and was the maid of honor at her wedding. And more recently I threw a thirtieth birthday party for her with her great crew of women friends. She has been there for me for important life moments too. I had a breast cancer diagnosis; she came to my final chemo session, and we celebrated together.

There is real satisfaction in seeing Jessica pay forward to her family all she's been given. Her developmental advances and her strengths and successes have benefited them. She's been an example to her siblings. One brother finished getting his college degree. A sister who is in her late twenties is working toward finishing school now. These days, Jessica is the wise one, their mentor. The agency she developed to get things done is priceless and remarkable.

Although she doesn't attribute all her success to having participated in the Big Brothers Big Sisters organization or to Deborah's mentorship, Jessica Walters acknowledges that Deborah was a big influence on her. Of all her siblings, she was the one who got the best grades, graduated college in four years, and started a professional life right after college. Her path was the most "normal" of all because she was able to avoid a lot of pitfalls that were challenges for the others. In providing the support of an attentive adult, Deborah taught her to consider the consequences of her behavior and guided her to navigate situations where she could have gone off track.

Research shows that many benefits flow from the mentorship of volunteers. Results in the wheelhouse of social-emotional learning—the development of soft skills such as self-confidence, self-efficacy, and goal setting—have been identified. And it is a fact, too, that parent-child bonds usually improve when a child is matched with a mentor. Jessica Walters's career has included serving as a caseworker for BBBS in central Illinois. She also ran an after-school program for second and third graders. Then she worked as the development and operations manager for Junior Achievement. With each new position, she built skills and changed lives. Today, she makes a big difference in the lives of children in her executive function for Big Brothers Big Sisters of Greater Cleveland. Her vision is to increase the scale of the program to reach more kids from hundreds of more households.

This story demonstrates the power of one volunteer helping one child reach her potential. Deborah's connection with Jessica gave her the strong foundation to continually pursue careers that have impacted more and more children, who may go on to help more and more children.

CHAPTER 19

A Journey of Resilience and Strength

The things you are passionate about are not random, they are your calling.
—Fabienne Fredrickson

When you are faced with challenges, there is nothing scarier than not knowing what the outcome might be. Time and again, I've heard stories from families and individuals that are nothing short of inspirational. They have picked themselves up, dusted themselves off, and—with the support, direction, and compassion given to them by volunteers—been able to find their inner strength that may have been suppressed by the overwhelming situations they temporarily found themselves in. It's not how many times you fall; it's how many times you get back up and keep going that will make forward progress.

Our volunteers embody the essence of community and shared humanity, standing as beacons of hope and assurance that no one has to navigate tough times alone. Through their selfless service, they demonstrate an essential truth: the burdens of life become more bearable when shared and lightened by the kindness of others. The support of volunteers transcends mere material assistance. It's an emotional lifeline, an affirmation of the value and dignity of every individual, regardless of their current circumstances. Ultimately, their commitment to alleviating the hardships of homelessness underscores the power of unity, compassion, and shared responsibility in transforming lives.

Jeff Armstrong, who is currently the executive director of Family Promise of the Midlands in South Carolina, understands the importance of human connection in helping people avoid or transition out of homelessness, because he himself was homeless off and on in his childhood and early teenage years. He has made it his personal mission to create programs for children in unstable households, like the one he lived in as a child, that give them access to the same experiences as their peers. For him, participating in athletics and interacting routinely with his teammates were instrumental in opening his mind to opportunities he would not have known about otherwise.

Because of his past, Jeff understands where the families he serves are coming from, including how resigned they may feel to their circumstances. But he believes this mindset can be shifted with support. There are lived experiences and meaningful encounters that can help youth bridge the gap between hopelessness and possibility, such as moments of curiosity when they think *What if?* and feel encouraged to reach for something more. This leads them to take steps that build stability.

JEFF

I don't do the work I do for awards or accolades. The purpose that motivates me is helping families by solving issues related to housing. Ever since I was a kid, I knew I wanted to be of service and to help young people. I grew up in Stockton, California, and moved with my parents to Virginia when I was about thirteen. I had an older brother who ran away when I was four. My father was a heavy substance user and abused my mother. He didn't work but would spend my mom's whole paycheck. And since he was in a constant state of spending, we were all in a constant state of need. This resulted in evictions and leaving places because we couldn't pay the rent that was due, sleeping in the back seat of our '91 Ford Escort and washing up in gas station bathrooms, sometimes moving in and out of motels.

That was the kind of life I knew growing up, and I thought it was normal until I saw differently. *Everybody goes through this, right?* I thought. I loosely knew my friends on the basketball team had it better than me—they lived in nicer neighborhoods, both their parents were working, and there wasn't the same level of trauma in their households.

One day, I came home from school to find out we were moving east. The thinking was that life would be better because my father's family was there. But after about a week living with my aunt, she cut us off, saying, "Look, I can't keep feeding you guys. I didn't think it would be like this." So we were back at square one. Fortunately, the faith community was good to us. My mom got a job as a secretary at a church, so we ate food from their food pantry. The family car was donated by the church. My dad stayed, and his health deteriorated until he died. At the end, my mother was basically his nurse. I was married and living in Maryland by then.

Going through the things families in our situation go through made me determined—like nobody's business—not to live the same chaotic way as an adult. The saddest part of poverty is the mindset. You're always dodging creditors, so you develop an "us against them" mentality. It's a generational curse. The mentality doesn't shift until you see for yourself how it feels not to owe anything to anyone and until you don't have to worry about making payment arrangements. My father never knew his own father, and he was cut off by his family. Through no fault of my own, I was caught up in a cycle as a child and a teen because of decisions others had made. Their addictions and the instability they caused created ideas in my mind like, *People don't care about me. They don't want to help me.*

Such concepts follow you around.

For a long time, I just shouldered the trauma I felt. Of course, I wanted to wear new and fancier clothes. But I didn't ever say, *Oh man, I have to wear the same thing again!* I moved forward, accepting what was. It is through lived experiences that we change our programming.

My basketball coach is someone I credit with being instrumental to the growth of my mindset. One winter morning, as I was waiting for a city bus to get to practice, I saw him drive by me at the bus stop. I waved and he waved back, but he didn't pick me up. Before practice, he called me over and said, "Son, do you know why I didn't pick you up this morning?"

I replied, "I have no idea."

And he said, "Because you didn't sign up for driver's ed."

I looked at him like he said something funny. "Well, Coach, why would I do that? Our family doesn't have a car."

In response, he said something like, "Never let what you don't have today impact your decisions about tomorrow." *Yeah right.* I was still bothered by him leaving me standing out in the cold. But as I thought more about his words, I decided I would sign up for that class. *We don't have a car, but what if? What if I need a license for something in the future?* He planted seeds in me like that.

My fourth-grade teacher was another person who helped me push for more in my life. She was young. She'd just graduated from college, and it was her first year teaching. I'll never forget it. I actually saw the baseball player Nolan Ryan pitch a no-hitter in Oakland in person on June 10, 1990. My teacher bought tickets for three students from my class, and we drove to the stadium to see the Oakland Athletics play the Texas Rangers. That was instrumental to my vision for my life. For years, I thought we were rewarded for being the smartest kids in class. It was only in looking back that I realized it was because she knew all of us had something going on in our homes. That game, seeing the field and those lights, being seated in the top rows of the upper deck at age ten, was magical. It was a major moment that impacted me greatly.

I feel responsible for paying it forward to the children in our program now. I'm super protective of our families as a whole, but I want kids to be exposed to all sorts of things that can inspire them. You never know what a moment is going to do for a child or where it might lead. A six-year-old is living in a house now. She never slept in her own bed in her own room before. Our volunteers send her letters because she loves getting mail. It builds trust in her mind that she's good enough and safe enough to do all kinds of things with her life.

I get indescribable joy when I see someone believe in themself in a way they never have, and to see the relief and trust in their eyes that everything is going to be all right.

Never in a million years would I have thought as a teenager that I would be speaking to different congregations on Sundays as I do now in my role for Family Promise. But here I am sharing this message with them, saying, "Listen, there could be one statement you make. It could be one word. It could be one note of encouragement you write. This makes a significant impact."

One of the moms in our program became a teacher. She went from working three jobs to getting a bachelor's degree and then to doing an unpaid internship. When in life has anyone done an unpaid internship without someone else, like a spouse or relative, supporting them? This mom became an elementary school teacher, and our volunteers and program were her support system. She is now pursuing a master's degree to teach special-needs children.

Some volunteers make a positive impact in the lives of others by teaching, coaching, or mentoring. While the act of donating our time may arise from a place of compassion, it can also bring about profound healing and understanding when we offer others the support we may have desperately needed at some point in our lives. Genuine conversations that stem from observing and caring deeply for someone's needs can unlock solutions that may have been previously hidden and lead them down a road of much-needed healing. If one avenue of giving back does not feel right, there are many other opportunities to explore.

CHAPTER 20

Keeping a Promise

> You may encounter many defeats, but you must not be defeated. In fact, it may be necessary to encounter the defeats, so you can know who you are, what you can rise from, how you can still come out of it.
>
> —Maya Angelou

As an organization deeply committed to preventing and ending family homelessness, Family Promise upheld its promise and became the nation's leader in this effort. But I'll never forget the encouraging, faith-filled words Irene said to me that day in the Bahamas: "You just wait and see what God is going to do through you and for you. You are going to help millions!"

While it's true I started something nearly forty years ago, it was our tireless volunteers—currently more than 200,000 nationwide—who contributed their time and energy to this noble cause. Collectively, we have helped more than a million individuals in need. We are still continually pushing the boundaries and working to help countless others who are still struggling. With 200 affiliates in forty-three states joining our cause, we have been able to provide homelessness prevention, shelter, transitional housing, affordable housing, and a host of other services and programs for families who may have once felt marginalized and forgotten.

It's humbling when people congratulate me on what I've achieved. And it was an honor to be invited to the White House in 1992 to receive the Annual Points of Light Award, championing the use of volunteers to help solve social problems and serve some higher purpose other than ourselves.

With the success of our program, I was very grateful for the appreciation shown to me at the White House, and I liked the idea of being a "Point of Light." They said it recognized "how one neighbor can help another while calling upon a nation to take action and service toward our fellow citizens." Nonetheless, I was also very aware it wasn't enough. If you had a million points of light, they still wouldn't be enough to solve the underlying social issues that cause poverty on one end of the social scale, and greed and corruption on the other.

We need the government to provide policies and to partner with nonprofits across the country to lift families out of poverty and homelessness. I don't believe that a country as rich as America, which contains so many good-hearted people, can't find a compassionate way to ensure that all of its citizens at least have a roof over their heads and decent food in their stomachs.

Today, in an era marked by rising income inequality, stagnating wages, and escalating cost of living, an individual working full-time at the federal minimum wage struggles to afford even the most basic necessities. There is no state in the

United States where a worker earning the federal minimum wage can afford a two-bedroom rental home at fair market rent by working a standard forty-hour week. This is just one stark illustration of the economic strain many Americans face, which can quickly lead to precarious housing situations and even homelessness.

Therefore, it is important to advocate for substantive policy reforms and facilitate partnerships between government and nonprofit organizations to alleviate poverty and homelessness on a broader scale. The reality is that no number of individual good deeds can replace the role of strong, equitable public policies in providing a stable safety net and fostering a more just society.

It's within our grasp as an affluent nation, replete with compassionate and dedicated individuals, to create a society where every citizen has access to fundamental human rights of a secure home and nourishing food. This is not merely a matter of economic policy; it is an ethical imperative that goes to the very heart of our shared values and aspirations for a more equitable and inclusive America.

When George W. Bush was president, he visited one of our affiliates in Ohio and praised our executive director for her outstanding work, stating, "Helping one heart, one soul at a time. God bless you." While we were grateful for the appreciation, the problem had grown way too big to be solved "one soul at a time" when it's growing bigger all the time.

When you spend time volunteering and listening to the stories of people who have fallen homeless, you will understand the terrible barriers they face. We need people to take care of our older people in nursing homes, but we expect those people to work for wages that keep them below the poverty line. While many enjoy the convenience of fast-food outlets, some of the people who serve us cannot afford to keep a roof over their heads due to their low wages. This is true with many others in jobs that pay minimum wage.

Homelessness isn't a political issue, and it's not a question of being a Republican or a Democrat. We have faced criticism from people on the left who think that by taking on responsibility for helping the poor, we are letting the government off the hook. They believe it should be the government's responsibility and not ours. My answer to them is that we can't sit by while individuals suffer and wait for someone else to solve it. If there is something we could be doing as individuals to alleviate the pain of people who are hurting right now, then we should do it.

Although my father didn't live long enough to see me go to the White House, he and my sister did see me receive a civic award. I watched his face as it was announced and saw his lip curl up a tiny bit, a sign I had learned to recognize meant he was proud of me. People would tell me he was always bragging about me, and he told Carol that I could "achieve anything I put my mind to." While it took time, I now know he loved me very much.

As for my beautiful baby sister, Carol, she was unsuccessful in her efforts to give up smoking. After going to the doctor because of pain in her shoulder, Carol found out she had small-cell lung cancer and was admitted to the hospital that day. I stayed with her, sleeping on a cot in her hospital room, but Carol died just two weeks after being admitted.

The loss of those we love hurts, so it's essential to value and show family, friends, and our fellow human beings as much love and compassion as we can while they are here with us.

When I resigned from my position as CEO of Family Promise in 2016, I was confident in the knowledge that I had identified a worthy successor to take on this significant responsibility. Claas Ehlers, who I had hired two decades before, was the perfect candidate and had an exceptional track record developing and overseeing new affiliates. His leadership would inspire meaningful change and drive the organization to new heights. After seven years as CEO, Claas stepped down, and we were fortunate enough to hire internally again. Cheryl Schuch, who was CEO of our Grand Rapids Affiliate, seamlessly transitioned to head the national organization.

Even after my retirement, I remained passionate about inspiring and motivating our volunteers and continued to speak on behalf of the organization. I looked forward to contributing in any way I could to the continued growth and success of Family Promise. In creating Family Promise, I had done more than I'd ever imagined. Yet, at that moment, I knew retirement was just a word—there was more to do!

CHAPTER 21

An Unbroken Spirit

> Challenges are gifts that force us to search for a new center of gravity. Don't fight them. Just find a new way to stand.
>
> —Oprah Winfrey

I had finally arrived at a place in my life where I could revel in the simple joys of spending quality time with my children and five grandchildren. For a few years, from 2016 to 2019, I was drawn to the tranquil shores of Miami Beach, where I was fortunate enough to have a cozy condo of my own.

On a particularly glorious day, February 12, 2019, I was lounging by the sparkling swimming pool, basking in the gentle warmth of the sun on my skin. In that idyllic moment, I couldn't help but feel overcome with gratitude for the blessings in my life—my family, my health, and the simple pleasures that bring me joy. As I paused to ponder my next move, I contemplated having lunch, followed by a massage. But first, I had an appointment for cryotherapy at the spa.

Cryotherapy is a cutting-edge therapy that uses extremely

low temperatures to promote healing and rejuvenation. I'd had cryotherapy about thirty times, both in Miami Beach and in Summit, New Jersey, and was used to the process. That day, when I arrived at my appointment, I casually inquired, "Who will be my attendant?"

The woman who ran the spa told me my attendant, a young woman, had only worked there for four weeks, but she assured me she was fully trained. I was okay with it, because I never had anything go wrong, and it took only a maximum of three minutes for the treatment. But this time, the chamber became colder than I'd ever known it to be. Afraid when I couldn't feel my body, I called out, "I'm cold. I'm so cold."

The attendant looked at me and, rather than standing in front of the door, she got behind the cryochamber, opening the door from the back before the usual time frame, and expected me to walk out. The usual practice, however, was that the attendant stood in front of the door to help you if needed, but since she was behind it, she couldn't help me out. When the attendant opened the door, I fell out like a popsicle, hitting the top of my forehead on a raised ledge where the wall and the floor met, and I started bleeding.

In an instant, anyone's life can change for many reasons, and that was the moment I felt my life change again. It reminds me of the short twenty-five minutes between leaving my mother for school and Maggie showing up to find my mother on the back lawn—ultimately ending her life and changing mine forever.

I was somehow completely composed, but everyone around me was screaming and yelling, "Oh my God!"

I barely managed to ask for a phone, which they held up to my mouth so I could speak with my sons, Brad and Doug.

Incredibly close with them, I explained that I didn't have any feeling from the neck down, and they immediately flew down to Miami to be with me. When the ambulance arrived, one of the EMTs said I was so cold that I was hypothermic. Once they got me ready to move, the EMTs had difficulty getting me out of the building on the gurney. Then they found the freight elevator and took me out of the spa. I already knew that certain parts of my body weren't responding or functioning properly.

Brad was at the hospital when I authorized the surgeon to operate on the back of my neck. My spinal cord wasn't completely severed—it was considered an incomplete injury. They warned us that time was critical, and I had none, so they immediately took me in to perform the surgery.

From the moment Brad arrived, and for twenty-seven days and nights, he was loving and attentive and stayed with me, sleeping by my side. This reminded me of my time spent with Carol, my sister, in the hospital, when she was dying of lung cancer. I didn't know what I would have done if I didn't have him. He didn't want me to see him cry, so he'd slip into the hallway, call his wife, Shelley, and cry to her. He said seeing his mother in this condition was the hardest thing he'd ever done. Doug also visited with me during that time. The overwhelming love and care I received from Brad, Doug, the rest of my family, and my friends was emotionally stirring.

When I returned to New Jersey after being in Florida, I spent a month in rehabilitation at the Kessler Institute in West Orange, New Jersey, renowned for its physical and occupational therapy. During that time, my sons sold my home and found a first-floor apartment for me near a park close to them. Aware my life had changed, I could no longer move and get around the way I had, but I didn't feel any anger toward the young woman for what had happened. And I never felt depressed. Why? It had everything to do with my spirit. My body is hurt, but my soul and spirit are not—and that's what keeps me going.

Initially after surgery, I couldn't feel my neck, but my condition has gradually improved since then. I can move my head and now have feeling and function in my legs, core, and left arm. Despite the path I must travel, which is for now in a wheelchair, life goes on. I've started painting again, and I exercise in a pool with a therapist's assistance. I have appointments for physical therapy, compassionate people taking care of me, and time with my family and friends; my life is good.

Being in a wheelchair has given me the time to slow down and appreciate how lives have been changed through Family Promise. I've learned more about how we impacted the lives of many in my time of reflection. When people say, "They treated me like family, not like a stranger," "They weren't judgmental and respected my dignity," and "They changed my life," I can really feel the depth of those words and the emotions behind them now. Before, our guests and volunteers would say the same things, but I was always so busy, running so fast to help the next family and the next, that it didn't fully sink in. Now that I'm not as mobile, I can feel the love and gratitude with a deeper understanding of how we have changed lives.

If you are a volunteer, I urge you to take the time to understand and care about the impact you're making on the lives of others. Imagine what it means to them and consider what it's doing for you.

Two weeks after the operation, the young woman who was my attendant at cryotherapy called to see how I was feeling. I told her I was doing better and let her know, "It's not your fault at all. You weren't properly trained." She told me she had been depressed for a while, but I believe the phone call helped, offering her some relief knowing I forgave her. It was something that happened to me, but it also brought me blessings. One is knowing that my body can be in pain sometimes and it can be broken, but *I cannot be broken.*

When a minister, Carletta Ashton, came to visit and asked me, "What have you learned from all this, Karen?" I said, "You know, you can break my body, but it doesn't break my spirit."

Today, I still go to the park, where I see Ed and other people around the pond. My compassion for helping people remains unwavering—I am incapable of retreating inward, ignoring the world around me. I continue to take care of Ed's phone bill, take him out to lunch, celebrate his birthday, and give him money when I see him. My efforts to reach out and help people and contribute to good causes have not waned. I go to events, such as the Kessler Foundation Stroll 'N Roll, to support those with spinal cord injuries, and despite my present circumstances, I'm still making wonderful connections. I talk to people within other organizations and their volunteers, and I remain engaged with Family Promise. That's what authentic compassion has taught me: you don't change who you innately are when your situation changes.

Despite what happened, I still have hope. It's what I want those experiencing homelessness or difficult times to have. I am trying to get into a study for my spine that could aid my mobility. Initially, my neck was in a brace, and I was in tremendous pain. Because I cannot walk, the individuals who assist with my home healthcare cannot slide me into my bed. Instead, I have to be placed into a Hoyer Lift, buckled in, and lifted onto the bed. It hurts, but I've gotten used to these new routines. Sometimes, I'm in pain, but I've gained an outsider's perspective, where I can receive things, compliments, and care from others. Although I cannot walk unaided, my mobility is improving, and I can take a few steps with the help of my physical therapist and a new walker device. I had gratitude before my injury, and I still have tremendous gratitude for everything God has used me to do and see.

Looking back on my life, I can see my spirit has been made stronger by my family, our guests, our volunteers, and all the selfless, compassionate people and organizations in this world. I know myself as Karen, a spiritual being. I challenge you to respect that we are all connected, take the path to your destiny, be a North Star for someone, see the problems in this world, instill hope, fulfill your longing, and have an expansive heart. I dare you to take a different road, find your Millie—your catalyst to be the change—be a kind individual, give someone a fresh start, and offer unexpected healing.

In your own special ways, help those in need, as your purpose is much greater than you think. You have more to contribute. Create a vision, open the doors, and change lives. Arm yourself with the power of compassion, allow your pain to have a silver lining, and make a promise to go beyond yourself. You have seeds of compassion within you, whether you know it or not. Allow yourself to experience the beauty of exploring those feelings. You will realize you are really doing something remarkable for yourself. Pay attention to what you care about or what tugs at your heartstrings. This is where you will find a bounty of compassion you can share. A compassionate gesture can be something as simple as sending a friend a text when you know it's their birthday, or acknowledging a friend or family member struggling with mental health.

Never underestimate the impact on the world around you of even the smallest action you take. If you have an inkling that you can make a difference, I encourage you to go for it with all your heart and soul. Your actions can have a ripple effect that spreads far beyond what you may have ever imagined. So don't hold back—embrace the power you have to make a positive change in the world and let your actions inspire others to do the same.

Choose to Make a Difference

If you want to contribute in some way and you're not sure where to begin, think about starting with small acts of kindness, whether in your own home, when you are out and about in your daily routine, or in your neighborhood. There are plenty of opportunities to reach out and help someone. You could:

- Reach out to someone who is having a tough time.
- Let somebody merge while in traffic.
- Cook meals for someone who is struggling.
- Hold the door for someone.
- Pay for the person behind you in the coffee line.
- Empty the dishwasher.
- Bring the garbage out for an elderly neighbor.
- Be kind to those who serve you.
- Leave a generous tip.
- Leave a gift bag for a new neighbor.
- Invite someone over for a holiday dinner if you know they are alone.
- Donate some of your gently worn clothes.
- Help an elderly person cross the street.
- Start a meal train for someone who is ill or for a new mother.

- Bring someone flowers.
- Take care of your friend's or neighbor's pet while they are away.
- Pay someone a compliment.
- Take someone's grocery cart after they've put their groceries in their car.
- Be happy for someone else's good fortune.
- Leave a kind note in public where someone may find it.
- Text or call someone to make sure they safely arrived at their destination.
- Put a Post-it note with a kind message on someone's windshield.
- Smile at a stranger.

Places Where You Are Needed

There are local organizations within your own community that could use your time, energy, or expertise. Looking on your town's website will give you an idea of what needs your community has. Your church, mosque, or synagogue may have outreach programs that you could assist with. It just takes a bit of asking around. There is always a need.

If you are looking to focus on a national organization, whether it helps people, the environment, or animals, you could search for a local branch.

- American Red Cross (www.redcross.org)

    - Headquarters: Washington, D.C.
    - The American Red Cross prevents and alleviates human suffering in the face of emergencies by mobilizing the power of volunteers and the generosity of donors. Volunteer opportunities available with the Red Cross can be helping with their blood drives, educating (e.g., teaching CPR), fundraising, or with their disaster services.

- American Society for the Prevention of Cruelty to Animals (www.aspca.org)

- Headquarters: New York, NY
- The ASPCA provides an effective means for the prevention of cruelty to animals throughout the United States. Volunteer through their pet adoptions, foster opportunities, animal rescues and rehabilitation, and government relations.

• Big Brothers Big Sisters (www.bbbs.org)

- Headquarters: Tampa, FL
- Big Brothers Big Sisters provides children facing adversity with one-to-one mentoring relationships that change their lives for the better. Mentor young people from age five through adulthood.

• Boys and Girls Club of America (www.bgca.org)

- Headquarters: Atlanta, GA
- Boys and Girls Club of America is a national organization of local chapters that provide voluntary after-school programs for young people. Help with homework, coach a game, teach an art project, and have a positive impact on the lives of youth.

• CASA (www.nationalcasagal.org)

- Headquarters: Seattle, WA
- The National CASA/GAL Association, together with state and local member programs, supports and promotes court-appointed volunteer advocacy,

so every child who has experienced abuse or neglect can be safe, have a permanent home, and have the opportunity to thrive. CASA serves 49 states and the District of Columbia.

- Catholic Charities (www.catholiccharitiesusa.org)

    - Headquarters: Alexandria, VA
    - Catholic Charities has 167 agencies nationwide that help people, regardless of their faith, who are struggling with poverty and other complex issues through its advocacy and disaster relief programs. Volunteers can visit nursing homes, help at a food pantry, fundraise, teach cooking, or mentor a child.

- Covenant House (www.covenanthouse.org)

    - Headquarters: New York, NY
    - Covenant House has 26 locations within the U.S. They provide workforce development and educational support, youth development services, legal service advocacy, and financial literacy programs for sixteen- to twenty-four-year-olds who are runaways or homeless.

- Family Promise (www.familypromise.org)

    - Headquarters: Summit, NJ
    - Family Promise is the nation's leading organization working to prevent and end family homelessness. It is currently in 43 states with 200 affiliates and

growing. Help with making meals, serve as an overnight host, meal delivery, financial literacy training, reading stories, providing companionship, creating resumes, or organizing supply drives.

- Feeding America (www.feedingamerica.org)

  - Headquarters: Chicago, IL
  - Feeding America is the largest hunger-relief organization in the United States. They are a nationwide network of 200 food banks, 60,000 food pantries, and community-based organizations in the U.S. Volunteers can work at a food bank, deliver meals, or sort and pack food.

- Habitat for Humanity (www.habitat.org)

  - Headquarters: Atlanta, GA (administrative); Americus, GA (operational)
  - Habitat for Humanity is a global nonprofit housing organization working in local communities across all 50 states in the U.S. Volunteers can help build a house, perform home repairs, or help out in the ReStore, where there are donated home goods to sell.

- Nature Conservancy (www.nature.org)

  - Headquarters: Arlington, VA
  - The Nature Conservancy is a global environmental nonprofit working to create a world where people

and nature can thrive. Volunteers can plant trees and remove invasive species at a nature preserve, participate in trash cleanup, help with data collection, and virtually volunteer using professional skills.

- Salvation Army (www.salvationarmyusa.org)

  - Headquarters: Alexandria, VA
  - The Salvation Army provides a range of social services and programs for communities and individuals throughout the world. Volunteers can help out in a shelter, organize food drives, or ring bells at a Red Kettle, along with many other opportunities.

Regardless of the manner in which you take action, looking outside yourself to be kind to someone, to help someone, to be part of changing someone's life not only is likely to benefit them, but you, too, will feel a change within you, satisfying that feeling of living a life fulfilled. Give the gift of volunteering.

Citations

1. "National Center on Family Homelessness," American Institutes for Research, accessed April 10, 2024, https://www.air.org/centers/national-center-family-homelessness.

2. "Children and Families," National Alliance to End Homelessness, updated December 2023, https://endhomelessness.org/homelessness-in-america/who-experiences-homelessness/children-and-families/.

3. "New HUD Data Show Dramatic Increase in Families and Youth in Homeless Shelters, Even While Significantly Undercounting Families and Youth Experiencing Homelessness," SchoolHouse Connection, published December 18, 2023, https://schoolhouseconnection.org/2023-hud-data/.

4. "Student Homelessness in America: School Years 2019–20 to 2021–22." National Center for Homeless Education. *National Center for Homeless Education*, https://nche.ed.gov/student-homelessness-in-america-school-years-2019-2020-to-2021-2022. Accessed 28 June 2024.

5. "Minimum Wage," U.S. Department of Labor, accessed

April 10, 2024, https://www.dol.gov/general/topic/wages/minimumwage.

6. "The Gap: A Shortage of Affordable Homes," National Low Income Housing Coalition (NLIHC), accessed April 10, 2024, https://nlihc.org/gap.

7. Peter J. Mateyka and Jayne Yoo, "Low-Income Renters Spent Larger Share of Income on Rent in 2021," Census Bureau, published March 2, 2023, https://www.census.gov/library/stories/2023/03/low-income-renters-spent-larger-share-of-income-on-rent.html#:~:text=Low%2DIncome%20Renters%20Hardest%20Hit,points%20higher%20than%20in%202019.

8. "What Does Living at the Poverty Line Look Like in the US?," USAFacts, updated September 18, 2023, https://usafacts.org/articles/what-does-living-at-the-poverty-line-look-like/.

9. Erik Gartland, "Chart Book: Funding Limitations Create Widespread Unmet Need for Rental Assistance," Center on Budget and Policy Priorities, published February 15, 2022, https://www.cbpp.org/research/housing/funding-limitations-create-widespread-unmet-need-for-rental-assistance.

10. Nick Tate, "Doctors Call for Single-Payer Alternative to Obamacare," published May 5, 2016, https://www.newsmax.com/Health/Health-News/single-payer-obamacare-alternative/201 6/05/05/id/727433/.

Acknowledgments

To Millie, who opened my eyes to people in need and inspired me to follow my heart.

To my family, who encouraged me all along the way.

To Jennifer Rustum, without her support, this book would not be possible. She did everything from writing, editing, researching, and so much more. No task was too big or too small.

I also would like to thank contributing writers Lou Aronica, Andrew Crofts, Stephanie Gunning, Jamie Heckelman, Creston Mapes, Nancy Peske, and Nadja Springer.

I want to thank Patrisha Simpson for her assistance with this project. And to all those who shared their stories with me through the years.

About the Author

Photo © Phil Cantor Photography

Karen Olson, the founder and CEO emeritus of Family Promise (www.familypromise.org), has dedicated her life to transforming the futures of homeless and low-income families. Her journey began in the mid-1980s when she first committed herself to the noble cause of advocacy for the disenfranchised and homeless. Garnering the power of human connection and community, Karen has since rallied more than a million volunteers nationwide, fostering an extensive network of support for the vulnerable. Also, because of all the efforts of the volunteers and staff, the organization has been able to assist over a million people experiencing homelessness.

Before her remarkable transition into the realm of social advocacy, Karen demonstrated her leadership prowess as a manager at Warner-Lambert. However, her leap into the world of nonprofit truly underscored her compassionate spirit and steadfast determination.

Over the years, Karen's efforts have been duly recognized, and she has received numerous awards. Some of them include President George H. W. Bush honoring her with the prestigious Annual Points of Light Award, and the New Jersey Governor's Pride Award recognizing Karen's remarkable social service contributions. The American Institute for Public Service also bestowed upon her the Jefferson Award, acknowledging her tireless public service efforts.

Karen Olson's relentless commitment to alleviating poverty and homelessness is a testament to her undying passion for social change.

Printed in the USA
CPSIA information can be obtained
at www.ICGtesting.com
LVHW092312250924
792139LV00011B/27